ISBN: 978-81-7541-405-1

First Published in India in 2008

New Public Management in India: Problems and Perspectives

Published by :
SHIPRA PUBLICATIONS
115-A, Vikas Marg, Shakarpur, Delhi-110092 (India)
Tel. : 91-11-65277210, 22500954, Fax : 91-11-22458662
Email : info@shiprapublications.com
www.shiprapublications.com

Preface

The volume deals with conceptual dimension, causes for the emergence of New Public Management, NPM as commercial, administrative and professional democratic partnership, reform process—no more and no less. It stands for lean government and learn administration. It also emphasizes a paradigm shift from conventional public governance to good governance through e-governance and qualitative improvement of public service systems. This collection of papers further deals with the implementation of NPM and its applicability in the governance of the country and sustainability, issues of innovation vs. accountability and merit vs. representativeness. Briefly, new model of public sector management is called 'Managerialism'. NPM market based public administration, Entrepreneurial government, thrust is toward a determined effort to implement the 3 Es: Efficiency, Economy and Effectiveness.

The NPM as is felt may destabilize the discipline of Public Administration. Because as a market driven model, NPM cannot solve the genuine problems of governance. There is also a doubt that the NPM might as well lead to high jacking of the state by the private and powerful. The public sphere may ultimately remain with the grass roots where people strive hard in their own way to build a democratic space away from the big state's massive management enterprise.

We thank all the scholars for contributing papers at the National Seminar on "Public Administration in India: Perspectives on New Public Management and Human Rights", organized by New Public Administration Society of India, Warangal,

Indian Institute of Public Administration, Mizoram Regional Branch, Aizawl and the Department of Public Administration, Mizoram University, Aizawl on May 05.07.2005.

New Delhi

R.N. Prasad, C. Lalkima,
S. Pathi, L.R. Tluanga,
L.N. Zovi, M.Lakshmi

Contents

I

Responsive Administration: India's Version of New Public Management

ARVIND K. SHARMA

If the 73rd and 74th Constitutional Amendments denote the political route to people's empowerment, India's Responsive Administration package—carrying diverse range of measures designed to induce a conscious citizen focus in civil service—might be thought to represent the managerial route to redefine power equations between the government and the citizen. India's 'responsive administration' initiative owes its inspiration to Britain's New Public Management (NPM). NPM's paternity can in turn be traced to the market-based public administration ideologies espoused by public choice theory, total quality management (TQM) movement and the re-engineering movement.

The larger ethos of the India's reform effort during the Nineties, in which the sentiment of equity dominated, was, however, shaped by two other intellectual orientations: the new public Administration movement and the Alternative Development paradigm.

The present chapter outlines India's 'responsive administration' initiative. This account is provided in the concluding section (section V) of the chapter. The preceding sections (sections I-IV) scrutinise and explore the forces that shaped the citizen-centric thrust of India's reform of the Nineties.

I. The Antecedents

The traditional means through which citizens seek to influence government decisions include the electoral system, political parties, legislators, pressure groups and the news media. Under the traditional model, civil service is made accountable to public through a set of hierarchical structures responsive to the ministers and legislators. Under this arrangement, politicians take care of the normative side of things by securing passage of legislations, which purportedly reflect popular will, whereas bureaucracy ensures that public policies are carried into effect. Public input into the policy process, under this model, is routed via the elected representatives; the citizen participation in governance is definitionally indirect.

The 'responsive administration' idea, on the other hand, is directed towards achieving a direct and an ongoing citizen participation in governance process. This is sought to be realised by instituting procedures that make it possible for citizens to scrutinise, monitor and evaluate delivery of public services on a day-to-day basis. Under citizens' charters, for instance, the recipients are empowered through dissemination of information on key operations connected with deliveries (such as service standards and specifications, response-time for various public transactions, and so on), to keep track of the functioning of the delivery system. Prior citizen knowledge of performance indicators makes it possible for the programme bureaucracy to receive feedback and offer response to the same on an ongoing basis.

The distinguishing feature, which it is possible to distil from current practice in the 'responsive administration' domain is its stress on the public administrator's propensity to respond to the citizens' needs as these may be gauged from a direct recipient-provider contact.

The idea *per se* is not new, but its pervasive, across the globe applications in the realm of public service delivery are certainly more recent.

In the United States, for instance, the term 'participatory democracy'[1] has been associated with a variety of grass-roots movements during the late sixties, when radical groups advocated participatory democracy to cure what they believed to be the unresponsiveness and repressiveness of the traditional decision-making mechanisms. Under the Office of Economic Opportunity Act of 1964, a number of federally sponsored programmes were started with the aim of eliminating poverty and enabling the poor to gain control over decisions affecting their lives through direct participation in operations of the organisations conducting them. A noteworthy feature of the initiative was that local agencies were required to recruit and train recipients of services as programme decision makers. The clients were thought to possess a unique perspective which, it was believed, needed to be recognised and incorporated in programme planning and administrative decision-making.

In North America and Western Europe, similarly, the term 'citizen participation'[2] has, since the 1960s, been used to refer to direct citizen involvement in policy process by means of advisory and consultative fora. An important contributory factor in the development of citizen participation idea was the perceived failure of bureaucracy to meet policy needs at the local level; equally, there was the assertion that the amateurs knew more about policy needs at any level than the professional administrator.

Citizen participation is different from regular means of indirect citizen participation (e.g., voting, interest-group activity) in that most citizen participation is at the regional or local level. Common forms are: (a) the citizen committee as an advisory group; (b) the citizen committee as a governing group; (c) the citizen as staff member of advisory boards (sometimes called para-governments); and (d) the neighbourhood government.

One taxonomy classifies participatory devices in the United States in four categories:[3] (a) official citizen committees, citizen groups, and special interest groups; (b) individual forms (e.g., voting, appeals, demonstrations); (c) techniques that facilitate participation through information collection (e.g., surveys, hearings); and (d) methods which induce participation through information dissemination (e.g., open government, 'hot lines'). A large number of 'special interactive techniques', which aim to stimulate a two-way citizen-government communication, have also been developed; these *inter alia* include arbitration, mediation, policy delphi and interactive cable television. Most of these techniques, it is noteworthy, involve communication of citizens with civil servants rather than with political leaders.

Canada's more promising initiatives for promoting citizen participation have included government sponsorship for formation of pressure groups to exert influence on behalf of the previously unrepresented or under-represented segments of population (consumers, environmentalists, poor); and creation of advisory bodies (boards and councils) containing citizens' representatives, which are supported by public funds.[4] Citizen participation movement did not, however, produce a particularly dramatic effect in the Western Europe, where, one commentator noted as late as 1978, most countries were "still making do with the hierarchic and authoritarian model of public administration"[5]

II. The Emerging Idiom

An agreeable fallout of the efforts to remodel the citizen-administration relationship has been to trigger a debate on the role of the citizen in the public realm. A recent writing[6] offers a normative portrayal in terms of three possible positions on a continuum citizen empowerment: citizen as a customer, citizen as an owner, and citizen as a co-coinvestor.

These metaphors may be dwelt upon briefly. The *customer paradigm,* borrowing from the total quality management movement, views public systems as producers and suppliers of services. These manufacturers will, as typically happens in private business, conduct client satisfaction surveys, develop service standards, establish customer complaint systems, and so on. The customer model, in this way, galvanises civil servants around the central theme of citizen satisfaction.

The customer model focuses on production in operation of government: how well it works, and how well it delivers. In doing this, it posits government as the main actor in the arena. Government acts; citizens react. The customer metaphor assumes that citizens are passive consumers of government services; they relate with government through transactions, surveys or complaints.

Under the customer metaphor, *the* citizens are, basically, low-involvement, self-interested consumers, and government drives and directs citizen-government relationship. Unlike this, under the *owner model*,[7] citizens are pictured as owners of the government enterprise (because they provide capital for the business; they produce revenue) and, as such, they must actively supervise its operations. Citizens are proactive, and it is they who drive and direct the relationship between government and citizens. The government, under this model, reacts.

The citizen's ownership role, however, tends towards sole proprietorship with its emphasis on individual responsibility for the enterprise. The proprietor defines and directs the scope of the enterprise and commands unilateral authority within the organisation. The proprietor's sway is unchallenged; he need not solicit opinion, seek consensus, or defer to democratic decision process. Insofar as this is so, the metaphor of citizen involvement, suggested under the model, is individually oriented rather than democratically or socially oriented.

While stressing the moral duty of citizens to accept responsibility for government, it is inconsistent with the ability or influence which most citizens may, in practice, have. "...in communities citizens behave more as shareholders with limited time, information, or expertise to influence government. Thus, citizens may have ownership rights in theory, but citizen-owners may find it difficult to relate to the owner model."[8]

In the third model of citizen-government interaction, citizens are pictured not as proprietors but *coinvestors* and shareholders while the government is a trustee.[9] The shareholder-trustee metaphor embodies important meaning with far reaching implications for the respective roles of the government and the citizen, and the citizens entitlements.

The implication of citizens being shareholders and not proprietors is that they are not individual owners of the government enterprise but coinvestors in a public trust, a community enterprise, or a common wealth. Citizen involvement is communally oriented; it involves co-partnership and co-ownership. Citizens have equal shares of ownership; consequently, they have access to equal benefits that flow from the community enterprise, such as public safety or legal protection from discrimination.

Government-as-trustee metaphor is also extremely significant A trustee, by definition, is one to whom property or possessions are legally committed in trust; the trustee does not own these possessions, only manages them on behalf of the shareholders. Under this model, government is a trustee and manager of assets, programmes and services that deliver incremental value to citizen-shareholders.

It is important to emphasise that, under the citizen-shareholder metaphor, the civil servants are not merely effective managers of the public assets; instead, their job as keepers of public trust has a special salience.

III. The Theoretical Foundations

Two influential theoretical orientations, in the Seventies, advanced in decisive ways the notion that the government needed to be made more responsive to the citizens than it had so far been. Both advocated decentralisation for citizen empowerment but each imparted its own meaning and flavour to the term and evolved its own methods to achieve decentralisation

Public Choice Theory

Public Choice Theory, oriented towards market values, argues that public agencies should compete to provide citizens with services instead of acting as monopolies. Since the citizen is a consumer of government goods and services, administrative responsiveness to individual citizen's demands would be increased by creating a market system for governmental activities. In the market system, the citizen-consumer will have the opportunity of choosing between competing service providers.

Policy implications flowing from public choice orientation relate to abolition of governmental monopoly over public service provision; introduction of markets in public service domain (introduce competing providers; competition will place bureaus in a state of permanent improvement); externalisation of production; and downsizing of bureaucracy. In the public choice school framework, introduction of market mechanisms into public services is the ultimate form of decentralisation, on the grounds that power, in theory at least, is decentralised to the individual service user who exercises choice between competing service providers.

The public choice argument on bureaucratic behaviour may be briefly outlined at the present juncture. The chief public choice emphasis is embedded in the assertion that the 'agents' which compel a customer focus in private sector are non-existent in government Budget is politically sponsored; revenue arises from periodic appropriations. Because revenues of government bureaus are unrelated to the volume and quality of transactions with service-users, they do not feel any compelling need to be responsive to the users' preferences and specifications. Business organisations are, on the other hand, self-correcting entities. Competition drives efficiency; keeps them in a state of 'permanent improvement' for otherwise they will be eliminated. Because government bureaus do not face such a threat, they are liable to become complacent; this breeds and supports an ethos of rampant wastes and inefficiency. In private sector, falling sales, dwindling revenues and declining profits administer timely warning signals to the firms; customer focus is inbuilt because sales/revenues/profits are directly dependent upon the patronage extended by the customers. Public agencies are not exposed to the disciplining influence of the market and are, therefore, inherently and inescapably inefficient, wasteful and unresponsive.

Three Public Choice perspectives on government bureaucracy are briefly presented below. Gordon Tullock is generally recognised as having produced the first sustained public choice analysis in his 1965 book titled *The Politics of Bureaucracy.*[10] Shortly thereafter, Anthony Downs subjected the bureaucratic behaviour to further scrutiny from a public choice standpoint in his book *Inside Bureaucracy,* which appeared in 1967.[11] In 1971, the public choice arguments about behaviour of bureau officials were drawn together and developed by William Niskanen in his book titled *Bureaucracy and Representative Government.*[12]

Gordon Tullock

Gordon Tullock's model of bureaucracy carries three principal emphases: (a) bureaucrats are motivated primarily be selfishness, (b) public agencies are not constrained by competition, and (c) their performance is difficult to monitor.

The prime mover of bureaucratic behaviour, Tullock asserts, is the official's desire to maximise their promotion prospects; desire to promote public interest is a consideration very much on the fringe. Selfishness in Tullock's perspective on bureaucracy implies, centrally, the notion of 'getting ahead,' 'moving up in the hierarchy.' The pursuit of promotion *per se* achieves primacy in a bureaucrat's scheme of things by virtue of political power and physical comfort to which such upward movement in hierarchy provides an access; the desire to move up should not be interpreted or described entirely in terms of creature comforts or large bank accounts, Tullock asserts.

This, Tullock argues, has its own consequences. Whereas, in a competitive market, merit (as reflected in the individuals ability to contribute to the organisation's performance) will form the basis of promotion, in government, because in a typical government bureaucracy there are no objective measures of performance, promotion depends on the bureaucrats' capacity to please their superiors. The result is concentration, near the top of the hierarchy, of individuals who are self-servers and whose ability to contribute to formal goals of organisation is suspect Inevitably, the effort towards organisational goal attainment is diluted.

The problem at the root of inefficiency which afflicts bureaus, Tullock argues, is that they are not subject to the disciplining influence of competition: they are monopolistic; the external check of competition that is present in business organisations is absent. "Government agencies can follow inefficient policies for very long periods without being eliminated.... The official is much less subject to pressure for efficiency than is the normal business manager. To the individual official, efficiency is meaningful not in terms of the organisation's goals, but in terms of his own." (Tullock: p. 68.)

In the absence of competition, good performance might be secured through a system of scrutiny of the results arising from the prevalent patterns of bureaucratic behaviour. This, however, poses its own problems in government: because of the absence of an unambiguous performance yardstick, like profit, it is difficult to institute an objective performance appraisal system. For the same reason, control and evaluation of individuals and agencies in the public domain remains an intractable problem.

Tullock concludes that much of modern bureaucracy is simply a mistake...continuing failures of bureaucracy are met in part by continuing reorganizations.... In part the failures are met by concealed shifts in the objectives of the organization.... The governmental bureau becomes the permanent fixture, with the objectives continually changing. Over time, the vested interests of the bureaucrats themselves become more and more important in justifying the organisation. (Tullock: p. 93.)

Anthony Downs

The fundamental premise of Anthony Downs' exposition is that bureaucrats, like all other agents in society, are motivated by their own self-interests. That, whereas in private firms, exposed to market discipline, such biases in individuals will be detected and checked through loss of sales and declining profits, in government agencies, pursuit of self-interest by public officials tends to become unrestrained because discipline imposed by competition, as well as profit motive, are absent.

The implication, broadly, of Downs' analysis is that, in public bureaucracies, the behaviour of officials will be primarily determined by considerations of power, prestige, money, security and convenience; and that, in the absence of a competitive environment, there is no means to channel essentially self-interested behaviour towards the fulfilment of public ends.

Downs further argues that it would be possible to check this, and the bureaucrats' private motives channelled towards public interest, if suitable institutional arrangements in the form of a robust system of monitoring could be put in place. He, however, expresses apprehensions regarding this principally on the grounds that monitoring agencies which may be established are themselves liable to become bureaucratised: over time monitoring agency itself becomes a bureau with activities that reflect the interest of its own staff; the volume and detail of reporting required by monitoring agencies tends to rise steadily over time regardless of the amount or nature of activity being monitored. Secondly, the organisation being monitored will itself incur costs in having to furnish the requested information. And, very importantly, the agency under scrutiny will expend considerable effort and resources in attempting to thwart, evade or counteract the monitoring agency. Downs labels it as the 'Law of Counter Control.'

To the problems that beset monitoring, Anthony Downs attributes the tendency for excessive growth which public agencies display. For a private firm, market for output (volume of sales leading to revenues) determines how much it may expand. Downs argues that all organisations have an inherent tendency towards expansion, but that this is specially pronounced in public systems because they do not receive revenue from customers who would pay voluntarily for their services. Essential problem therefore is that 'market for output" of a bureau does not serve as a check on its expenditure growth; on the contrary, a defining characteristic of the bureau is that its income is provided by political sovereigns on behalf of the tax payers.

Downs points to the following effects of bureaucratic expansion.

Excessive size becomes a form of protection against abolition. As they grow older, bureaus become less responsive to new needs. While all organisations become conservative, as they get older, this is particularly true of bureaus because they are insulated from competition.

Size mediates against proper coordination and control. Downs labels this as the 'law of diminishing control' and the 'law of decreasing coordination.' The result, typically, is that a significant portion of the bureau's activity tends increasingly to become unrelated to its formal goals.

As bureaucracy grows, the efficiency of resource utilisation falls. Downs argues, intuitively it can be postulated that the total amount of waste and inefficiency in society would rise as bureaucracy becomes more prominent. Because waste is harder to define and detect in bureaus than in private firms. There are, moreover, no automatic mechanisms (as in the latter) for limiting waste in public organisations. The general conclusion, to which Downs is driven by this analysis, is that the society would be better off in arranging to have services produced by market oriented organisations rather than bureaus.

William Niskanen

A defining feature of government bureaus, William Niskanen states, is that their revenues are provided enbloc by political sponsors (the ministers); that bureaus are, definitionally, financed by a periodic appropriation. The result is that civil servants tend to be indifferent to the interests of customers because the departments' own revenues are not dependent upon the customers. Secondly, public officials remain disinterested in minimising costs and maximising profits, since they do not make a personal financial gain from the difference between revenue and cost of supplying services.

Besides, William Niskanen asserts, bureaucrats display a budget-maximising behaviour, since the variables that enter their utility function (viz., salary, perks, public reputation, power, patronage, etc.) are dependent upon the size of the budget their departments command.

The effect of budget-maximising behaviour, Niskanen concludes, inevitably is the oversupply of public service provision so that expansion of the bureau and that of staff and equipment, as well as claims for enhanced future budgets, could be justified. Besides, there is a higher per unit cost of producing services, since no part of any 'efficiency saving' accrues directly to bureau staff. And, for the same reason, there is no incentive to economise on the tax-payers' money.

Alternative Development Paradigm

The enunciators of public choice orientation advocated a market-based approach to decentralisation. More or less parallely, during the Seventies, was developing a diametrically opposite approach to decentralisation in the form of

'Alternative Development' paradigm, whose advocates stressed that, under the traditional modernisation model, the contours, contents and consequences of development were being dictated by a powerful, self-serving oligarchy, consisting of the political elite, bureaucracy, entrepreneurs, rich peasants, professionals, and so forth. That this capital-centred, non-participatory model had led to a highly inequitous pattern of development which had reduced an overwhelming majority to a state of stark poverty.[13]

The argument which was developed was that the phenomenon of mass poverty was embedded in and arose from the state of disempowerment to which the teeming millions had been reduced. That powerlessness—lack of voice in political processes and fora—was a critical dimension of poverty. That this powerlessness manifested itself in an inability to control the forces which determined access to resources and opportunities. In terms of this interpretation, poverty was identified as being structural in nature. The task of removing poverty, therefore, entailed a reordering of the societal power equations in such a way that the society's oppressed, pushed to the margins of the political arenas where battles for resources and opportunities are fought, were brought to the centre-stage of the governance process. This was an argument for fostering participation of the poor in the society's power structure and for a realignment of the societal power equations in favour of the oppressed and the excluded. Participation in the Alternative Development—also called the 'People Centred' Development—framework is equated with the process of redistributing political power to enable the society's poor and under-privileged sections to achieve access to resources they previously lacked. It seeks the formation of a countervailing force to confront the established power configurations in given contexts; this has been characterised as the process of 'creating space' within which the vulnerable groups might begin to function and to take action. This 'space to act' is critical for initiating 'structural change' or achieving a redistribution of assets in society. In other words, the paramountcy of structural change implies the need to take action, and this action can only be taken from a position of power.

This redistributive-politics-logic translated overtime into a powerful advocacy of political devolution, revitalisation of local self-governing institutions, empowerment of the local communities, grass-roots activism, user control, and so on. This line of thinking, espousing collective political action and citizenship development as a means to extract bureaucratic response, has over the years forged into a powerful advocacy of local democracy and a thorough revamp of the existing local self-government structures.

The essential import of the two intellectual orientations, recounted in the preceeding pages, lay in supplying a comprehensive logic to support a redefinition of the government-citizen relationship; even though the espousal of the citizen's cause, under each, is based on different, even antagonistic, ideological positions and leads to radically different policy prescriptions. The point to assert essentially is that the Seventies became a watershed; the core beliefs of Public Choice Theory and die Alternative Development idea served to trigger a paradigm shift. It was their arguments that became the basis for the assertion that the 'client' did not have to live on government's charity; that the 'citizen' had inalienable rights and entitlements vis-à-vis the government. The helpless, dependent 'client' through a process of transition was to have been transformed into the 'citizen' who would assert, who knew his claims, who was self-aware, who was in fact sovereign.

Total Quality Management

Advocacy of the rights of service-users vis-à-vis the providers in fact received much reinforcement from yet another source: the Total Quality Management (TQM) movement.[14] TQM's intellectual origins lay in the United States. It was the efforts of American engineers and statisticians, during the Second

World War, towards quality improvement in the domain of armament manufacturing which constituted the beginnings of what in the course the next decades developed into a body of beliefs and practices subsumed under the acronym TQM. W. Edwards Deming and Joseph M. Juran have been among the early exponents, the founding fathers, of the TQM philosophy. Philip Crosby and Tom Peters are the 'new wave' American TQM gurus of the Nineties. The intervening three decades were dominated by the Japanese; K. Ishikawa, G. Taguchi and Shigeo Shingo took the development of TQM dramatically further.

Customer satisfaction through continuous quality improvement forms the central emphasis of TQM philosophy. Quality consciousness, the urge to strive for quality, must, however, pervade the entire organisation in order that its quality-development effort may be sustained over time. From this derives the second principal emphasis of the quality movement, namely, the organisation's endeavour to remain client-focused shall succeed only to the degree it successfully harnesses every bit of ingenuity of its own constituents. Operationally, this translates in the need to empower the employees through strategies designed to secure a broad based employee participation and involvement in organisational decision making. In these terms, sensitivity to customer needs and a conscious employee focus form the two defining pillars of TQM.

The core concept of TQM, which lends it a generic applicability across occupational sectors, is that of process control: elimination of quality-defeating variations in the processes which deliver the end-product/service to the user/citizen. It concomitantly implies a continuous enhancement of the processes so as to eliminate waste, reduce costs and enhance efficiency. A philosophic commitment to the idea of never-ending improvement in quality is the touch-stone of TQM thinking. Quality, as Philip Crosby puts it, is not 'goodness' or 'elegance', it is instead conformance to the requirements of the customer. TQM, it has been argued, is innately customer-driven also in that the approach offers a framework for integrating customer feedback on a continuous basis which permits an ongoing refinement of the processes involved in producing and delivering services.

A widely shared assumption in the TQM thinking is that quality builds incrementally through efforts of individuals performing discrete activities of which the specific processes might be composed. Every single step in the process is viewed as an opportunity for eliminating error and enhancing quality, which leads to the quality teachers' assertion that those closest to the processes should be made responsible for introducing improvements in them. This approach stands in a sharp contrast to the traditional thinking, under which the arch-definers of quality were designated as 'quality-controllers' to be summoned for the job when the process was virtually over; and where there was no invitation for the rank-and-file workers to analyse and control their own work processes to eradicate error, or devise for themselves a whole new process and, thus, make their contribution towards quality enhancement. Under TQM, on the other hand, quality is thought to be a seamlessly pervasive process in which all, from top to the bottom of hierarchy, are involved. For sustaining a quality-driven involvement on that scale, the work culture will need to be metamorphosed to secure what a Japanese TQM advocate describes as the "day-to-day mobilisation of every ounce of intelligence" within the organisation.

IV. New Public Management

Since the Eighties, the OECD (Organisation for Economic Cooperation and Development) countries have witnessed a widespread reform of their public bureaucracies induced by the prescriptions of Public Choice Theory. This has been pursued under the rubric of New Public Management (NPM), an expression coined by British Observers to refer to a wholesale incorporation into the public domain of the core values identified with private sector that brought about a dramatic transformation of the traditional administrative practice.[15]

The principal features of NPM include:[16]

— an emphasis away from issues of policy to those of management;
— a shift towards the disaggregation of administrative units;
— the creation of explicit standards and measures of performance;
— an emphasis on results rather than procedures;
— the use of contract arrangement inside as well as outside the public sector;
— the promotion of competition within public sector; and
— a general adoption of private sector corporate practices.

National Performance Review (NPR) is the Clinton Administration's version of New Public Management.[17] Administrative reform was on Clinton's agenda even before he was elected. Clinton based his proposals for reform, during the election campaign, on Osborne and Gaebler's *Reinventing Government* (1992) in which the authors envisage a new form of entrepreneurial government with increased competition in service delivery, devolved budgets allocated on the basis of outcomes, and community oriented service provision. Their vision is based on the idea that, in many cases, policy decisions can be separated from service delivery: 'steering' can be separated from 'rowing', whereby government becomes a catalyst empowering communities to solve their own problems. *Reinventing Government is* based on experiences from the United States' state and local governments; for the same reason it does not tackle the scale or scope of problems found in the US federal government. Perhaps it was this realisation that led Clinton to initiate NPR, an intensive six-month study of the federal bureaucracy carried out by 250 government employees under the leadership of *Vice* President, AI Gore.

NPR, of which there were two phases[18]—the first occurring in 1993 and the second in 1995—had, in its first phase, focused primarily on how government should work, not on what it should do. Three themes on which it concentrated were: (i) Putting Customers First, (ii) Cutting Red Tape, and (iii) Empowering Employees To Get Results. Privatisation, a prominent theme in most NPM reforms of the 1980s, was noticeably absent from NPR-I (a cryptic characterisation of phase one). Phase two, announced in 1995, presents a contrast, with privatisation and contracting out brought to the fore. NPR-II concentrated on 'Cutting Back to Basics', which has come to mean a refocusing and, particularly, a downsizing of federal government activities. This is sought to achieved by following methods:

(i) Service termination: meaning that a particular service need not be provided by federal government any more.
(ii) Privatisation: implying sale of assets by federal government.
(iii) Quasi-Government Corporations: instead of providing the service directly as a public good, government creates a corporation.
(iv) Creation of public-private partnerships: where the government may share in ownership of assets and may share in operational responsibilities.
(v) Competition: which is the contracting-out or outsourcing alternative.

When an integrated view of the two paradigmatic shifts—the application of market concepts to public administration and shift in development thinking—is taken, one discovers a rich harvest of administrative reform movements across the globe with multiple emphases, of which two stand out more prominently. The countries in question are focusing not merely on questions of economy and efficiency; the reform is instead being viewed as a means to achieve a fundamental reordering of the power equations between the providers and the recipients of public goods and services so as to put the latter decisively in control. The power realignment question makes a dominant presence in the reform agenda. This emphasis, the advocates of reinventing government have cloaked in the phrase 'customer-driven bureaucracies'. The National Performance Review underlines it in its 'customer-first' phrase. The protagonists of New Public Management underscore the paramountcy of checking the forays of the Administrative Class in the realm of policy through the formation of executive agencies which are contracted by their parent departments to provide specified services. This on the ground that a civil service confined to a managerial role, which is defined by a performance agreement and supported by requisite operational freedom, will be more responsive to public needs and aspirations.

India, in tune with the people's empowerment philosophy, expounded in the momentous 73rd and 74th Constitutional Amendments, and inspired by the profoundly influential NPM and NPR initiatives produced, in the second half of the Nineties, its own version of the civil service reform. The label that has gained currency in referring to the different strands and nuances of the reform is 'Responsive Administration'. The 8-page Discussion Note (titled *An Agenda For Effective and Responsive Administration)* framed by the Union Government's Department of Administrative Reforms and Public Grievances for the November 20, 1996 conference of chief secretaries may be thought to constitute an officially authenticated statement of the scale and scope of the Indian reform. The major highlights include the document's emphasis on the need to define development more inclusively than merely in economic terms, the urgency which it attaches to the task of bringing the society's weaker sections to the center stage of the governance process, and its strident advocacy of the professionalisation of the HRD domain in government. The chief secretaries' conference was followed by the chief ministers' conference, in May 1997, where the proposals emanating from the 1996 conference of the chief secretaries were endorsed. The statement adopted at the chief ministers' conference is, very significantly, titled as the "Action Plan for Effective and Responsive Administration". The measures listed in the Action Plan have since been taken up for implementation by the union as well as the state governments.

The following section portrays the scope of the 'Responsive Administration' package at the Union Government level; it merely catalogues the major initiatives of the Central Government as these have unfolded in the wake of the two conferences.

V. India's Reform Package

The Indian initiative may be thought to have two distinct dimensions.

The first of these involves measures to revitalise the local democracy. This has been sought to be achieved through an ambitious plan of political devolution under the rubrics of 73rd and 74th Constitutional Amendments. The aim is to provide a larger political space to local communities in the country's governance; and, in particular, to empower the society's oppressed and excluded sections.

The second, with which we shall be concerned in the present section, involves measures directed at achieving a reform of the country's bureaucracy. This is, actually, a comprehensive reform package designed to streamline delivery systems, foster transparency and openness in public transactions, allow citizens an easy, unhasseled access to public services, improve the quality of citizen-administration interface, and, ultimately, realign the provider-recipient power equations to the citizen's advantage so as to augment the prospects of an accountable and responsive governance.

This, therefore, is a multi-faceted plan of action, involving a diverse range of initiatives impinging upon the responsiveness question. Three sets of measures are discernible in this managerial reform package. While admittedly there is an element of overlap as regards the concern(s) a particular component addresses, for the sake of academic understanding these may nevertheless be classified in separate categories, as follows: (i) accountability-fostering measures, (ii) measures for promoting transparency and openness, and (iii) measures directed at civil service performance and integrity.[19]

Bureaucratic Accountability

This category comprises: (a) introduction of citizen's charters, (b) measures to strengthen and streamline procedures for redressal of public grievances, and (c) steps directed at reviewing the existing legislations, rules and procedures; the exercise is essentially aimed at establishing or rationalising 'frameworks' for responsive governance. While these measures are recounted, mention in the passing may be made of the union government's efforts towards enacting the Lokpal Legislation.

Transparency and Openness

The 'freedom of information' Legislations form the crowning feature in this category. Freedom of Information Acts have been legislated in some of the states. At the centre, the Freedom of Information Act is yet to be enacted.

Other initiatives by central ministries in regard to transparency and openness, which have become operational, include the following two.

The first involves computerisation of departmental operations. The aim is three-fold: (a) facilitate tracking of receipts and files; (b) ensure easy public access to requisite information; and (c) promote inter-agency and intra-agency coordination.

The second concerns measures to secure a wide dissemination of information. These include recourse to user-guides, publications, notice-board displays, and so forth. Besides, information and facilitation counters (IFCs) in various ministries have also been set up. The IFCs provide information to users regarding the scope of activities of the concerned organisation, the schemes it operates, stipulated procedures to be followed, the status of applications, etc. All IFCs are computerised; and these are located outside the security zone to obviate the need, on the part of the visitor, to obtain an entry-pass.

Civil Service Performance and Integrity

Initiatives in this category include the following: (i) measures to curb corruption, (ii) efforts towards evolving a civil service code of ethics, (iii) contracting out of public services, and (iv) steps towards simplification of procedures.

In the ensuing pages, we shall briefly dwell upon some of the major initiatives under category-I (Accountability Fostering Measures) and category-III (Civil Service Performance and Integrity Related Measures).

Accountability Fostering Measures: Citizen's Charters

The concept of citizen's charter seeks basically to promote the idea of citizens' entitlements vis-a-vis the government: entitlement to easy, unhassled access to public services, to services of a stipulated quality and specifications, to efficient and courteous delivery, to a transparent conduct on the part of the provider, and so forth. The Central Government has commenced a phased introduction of citizen's charters in various ministries and their attached and subordinate offices. Basic concerns addressed by charters may be indicated presently. The citizen's charters:

(a) incorporate a statement of services a department offers;
(b) indicate service standards and remedies available to users in the event that there is a non-compliance with stipulated standards;
(c) insist on display of the requisite procedures and costs involved in obtaining the desired services;

(d) provide a structure for obtaining user feedback;
(e) institute easy-to-follow procedures for complaints and time-bound redressal of grievances;
(f) indicate response-time for various public transactions;
(g) set up machinery for system-audit, performance monitoring and independent agency evaluation.

Measures to Strengthen Internal Grievance-Redressal Machinery

Measures to strengthen internal grievance redressal machinery have been initiated by various ministries/departments of the central government. These *interalia* include the appointment of a grievances officer; institution of a grievances-analysis system for identifying major grievance-prone areas; observance of a meetingless day every week to ensure ready access of functionaries for grievance redressal; obligation to acknowledge grievance petitions, and their time-bound disposal; decentralisation of grievance redressal process to the lowest possible field formations; establishment of single-window system; and reinforcement of feedback and monitoring mechanisms.

Public Grievances Monitoring System

A Public Grievances Monitoring System (PGMS), devised by the Department of Administrative Reforms and Public Grievances, has been made available to all central ministries, and the same is currently operational. The PGMS is a uniform software which has been prepared with the help of National Informatics Centre for online monitoring of public grievances in the central ministries. Based on grievance codes formulated by the respective ministries, the PGMS enables online transmission of monthly statistics, from each ministry, pertaining to grievances received, disposed and pending. These are arranged department-wise, code-wise and age-wise (showing period of pendency).

Cabinet Secretariat's Directorate of Public Grievances

The Directorate of Public Grievances (DPG), functioning under the Cabinet Secretariat, discharges a grievance-redressal role in regard to the most grievance-prone ministries, e.g., railways, posts, telecommunications, banking division (under DEA), and regional passport authorities (under MEA). The DPG can call for files to ascertain if the grievances have been dealt with, by the concerned ministries, fairly and justly. The recommendations which the DPG may choose to make in particular cases carry enormous weight.

Nodal Officers/Directors of Public Grievances

Nodal Officers/Directors of Public Grievances have been appointed to oversee the disposal of grievances. They have been vested with powers to call for relevant files and take decision thereon with the approval of the appropriate authority. Agencies using this method include public sector banks, ministry of labour, department of supply.

Banking Ombudsman

Reserve Bank of India's Banking Ombudsman Scheme applies to all commercial banks whether incorporated in India or abroad for resolution of complaints relating to non-observance of the RBI directives on interest rates (or any other specified matter) and delay in disposal of loan applications.

The complainant may make a complaint to banking ombudsman if his representation (to the bank) has been rejected or response thereto delayed beyond two months, or if the complainant is otherwise not satisfied with the response. The banking ombudsman may make a recommendation after considering the circumstances of the case. If the recommendation is not acceptable to the complainant, the ombudsman shall announce an award after affording the concerned parties reasonable opportunity to present their case.

The Postal Department Initiatives

Because they have a large and on-going interface with public, the postal department has emerged with innovative concepts and devices for handling public grievances. These among others include the following:

(a) Appointment of 'Public Relations Inspectors' (PRIs) to monitor the delivery of unregistered mail.

(b) Introduction of 'Dak Adalats', for an on-the-spot redressal of complaints relating to delayed deliveries and indifferent counter-services. Dak Adalats have been in operation since 1990.

(c) Introduction of 'Post Forum', which is a local-level advisory body. Post fora, consisting of representatives of users (trade, commerce, industry, bulk-mailers), social workers and prominent citizens, have been constituted in three major post offices of each postal circle within the country. Post forum discusses all matters concerning the post, whether or not they may fall within the powers of the post master; cases outside the postmaster's purview are referred to the next higher authority. The practice of Post Forum was introduced in 1990.

(d) A 'Social Audit Panel' (SAP) was created in 1992. The SAP was established to provide inputs for evaluating the impact of telecommunications and postal facilities, particularly in the rural and semi-urban areas. The Panel consists of chairman, a convener and three members. The scope of the SAP's concerns is wide ranging. These include:

(i) social cost-benefit analysis of postal services;
(ii) analysis of loss-making postal services;
(iii) identifying leakages in the postal system; and
(iv) augmentation of the volume and quality of the existing

postal services. In making its recommendations, the SAP takes into consideration (a) whether the benefits are actually percolating down to the target group; (b) whether the available resources are being utilised in an optimum manner; and (c) whether the present structure is equitable and productive.

Civil Service Performance and Integrity-Related Measures

Measures Against Corruption

Important initiatives of the Central Government in the realm of corruption since the 1996 Chief Secretaries' Conference include: (i) the establishment, in PMO, of a Unit to monitor agencies dealing with corruption; (ii) initiation of steps to process the Vohra Committee report; (iii) vigorous monitoring of corruption cases, time-bound completion of disciplinary proceedings, including action towards compulsory retirement of civil servants of a doubtful integrity; and (iv) special drives against corruption, including surprise-raids and traps-laying.

Code of Ethics

While regulations to govern the conduct of the civil servants have been in existence both at the Centre as well as in the states, these are in the nature of formulations of do's and don'ts and do not represent a positive statement of values and beliefs. Accordingly, the Ministry of Personnel, Public grievances and Pensions have emerged with a draft 'Code of Ethics' which, having been endorsed by the Chief Ministers' conference, is presently being given a legal shape.

The Code prescribes, for civil servants, standards of integrity and conduct in diverse realms—

1. Interface with citizens should be characterised by civil servants' easy accessibility, and accountability, to be gauged with reference to yardsticks like quality of

service, timeliness, courtesy, freedom from bias, and so on.

2. The Code emphatically underscores the paramountcy of the civil servants' commitment to the (values enshrined in the) Constitution and the rule of law and casts on her/him the obligation to refuse to carry out unlawful commands of the superiors. It, equally unambiguously, extols the virtues of civil service neutrality by exhorting public servants to assist the duly constituted government in carrying out its business without being in any way influenced by the consideration of its political ideology.
3. To foster professionalism, the Code of Ethics enjoins civil servants to extend support to the juniors to resist illegal directives, reward good work and punish any dereliction of duty. The civil servants are asked to desist from contacting politicians and bringing peer pressure in service-related matters; and from abusing their official position to benefit themselves and others. The Code enjoins government functionaries to resist attempts to fragment the society and the civil service on caste and communal lines; not to unauthorisedly release information received in confidence, which may compromise privacy of an individual; and desist from public criticism of government policies.

Outsourcing of Services

In the wake of the chief secretaries' conference, a broad consensus appears to have emerged in favour of outsourcing peripheral and support services. Its advocacy has rested on familiar grounds: this will permit government to concentrate on its core functions; contracting out of services will help to right size a bloated bureaucracy; and it will help to bring about enhanced productivity. The areas of outsourcing recommended by the Fifth Central Pay Commission include construction and maintenance of government offices, residential colonies, factories and railway stations; housekeeping; sanitation; postal delivery; printing; computer-related services; apart from others.

However the restrictive provisions of Contract Labour (Regulation and Abolition) Act, 1970 come in the way, as was revealed when CPWD and Department of Health initiated measures to outsource some services jobs to private parties. Accordingly, on the initiative of the Department of Administrative Reforms and Public Grievances, a core group—headed by secretary (personnel) with secretary (labour), secretary (expenditure) and secretary (department of legal affairs) as its members—has been constituted to deal with the problem.

Recommendations of the Core Group have been to the following effects:

(a) Existing notifications, prohibiting engagement of contract labour, may be, where necessary, reviewed, modified or annulled.
(b) The exemptive provision under Section 31 of Contract Labour (Regulation and Abolition) Act may be permitted to be used more liberally till such time as the Act is amended. Eventually, the Core Group recommends, the existing Act may be amended to facilitate outsourcing
(c) A separate legislation, regarding contracting out of services by government departments, may be framed.

Simplification of Procedures

For making the system transparent and to ensure enforcement of accountability, a comprehensive revamp of the existing procedures, including an exercise designed to achieve simplification of the different variety of 'forms' in use by various ministries, has been commenced. To ensure that the ministry-level review of procedures was vigorous, the Department of Administrative Reforms and Public Grievances issued a set of Guidelines, in December 1996, whose principal emphases are as follows:

(a) To enable the customer to establish that he had filed an application before the concerned authority, there should be provision for a counterfoil/acknowledgement in the form.

(b) There should be provision for an on-the-spot scrutiny of the forms to ensure that if there might be deficiencies the customer is advised there and then.

(c) Documents to be furnished in support of an application should be listed in the form.

(d) There should be adequate space in the application form to accommodate information required to be furnished so as to obviate the need to attach loose sheets which are liable to go astray.

(e) The status of an application should be periodically intimated to the customer; for this as well as for processing information on public grievances, ministries must take recourse to computers.

(f) The ministries must review their working-days and working-hours to ascertain if these are convenient for their customers.

The Ministry of Administrative Reforms and Public Grievances specifically notes certain other basic omissions in the forms currently in use in government.

(a) Forms offer no guidance to customers regarding who may be approached in the event of delay, sub-standard service or harassment.

(b) Forms do not specify time period for filing complaints nor indicate documents required for processing complaints.

(c) Forms are silent on the compensation or relief admissible in the event of service failure or customer harassment.

NOTES AND REFERENCES

1. Ralph, C. Chandler and Jack, C. Plano, *The Public Administration Dictionary,* New York, John Wiley & Sons, 1982, p. 83.
2. *Ibid.,* p. 161.
3. Kenneth, Kernaghan, "Evolving Patterns of Administrative Responsiveness to the Public," *International Review of Administrative Sciences,* Brussels, Vol. 52, No. 1, January-March, 1986, p. 295.
4. *Ibid.,* pp. 96-97.
5. *Ibid.,* pp. 95-96
6. Gerald, E. Smith and Carole, A. Huntsman, "Reframing the Metaphor of the Citizen-Government Relationship," *Public Administration Review,* Vol. 57, No. 4, July-August, 1997, pp. 309-318.
7. This conceptualisation is attributed to Hindy Lauer Schachter ("Reinventing Government or Reinventing Ourselves: Two Models For Improving Government Performance," *Public Administration Review,* Vol. 55, No. 6, November-December, 1995, pp. 530-537).
8. Smith and Huntsman, *op. cit.,* pp. 312-13.
9. This has been enunciated by Smith and Huntsman, *ibid.*
10. Gordon Tullock, *The Politics of Bureaucracy,* Washington, DC, Public Affairs Press, 1965.
11. Anthony Downs, *Inside Bureaucracy,* Boston, Little Brown, 1967.
12. William Niskanen, *Bureaucracy and Representative Government,* Chicago, Aldine-Atherton, 1971.
13. For a critique of the classical development model, and a discussion on the Alternative Development thinking, *see* Rajani Kanth (Ed.), *Paradigms in Economic Development: Classic Perspectives, Critiques and Reflections,* New York, M.E. Sharp, Inc., 1994.
14. For a detailed commentary on various aspects of TQM, *see* Colin Morgan and Stephen Murgatroyd, *Total Quality Management in Public Sector: An International Perspective,* Buckingham/ Philadelphia, Open University Press, 1994.
15. Patrick Dunleavy, "The Globalisation of Public Services Production: Can Government be 'Best in World'," in Andrew Massie (Ed.), *Globalisation and Marketisation of Government Services: Comparing Contemporary Public Sector Developments,* London, Macmillan Press Ltd., 1997, p. 24; Andrew Massie, "In Search of the State: Markets, Myths and paradigms," in *ibid.,* p. 7.

16. *Ibid.*, p. 8; Danny Burns, *et al.*, *The Politics of Deconcentralisation,* Macmillan, 1994, p. 84.
17. Helen Margetts, "The National Performance Review: A New Humanistic Public Management," in Andrew Massie, *op. cit.*, p. 47.
18. For a description, *see ibid.*, pp. 51-70.
19. The description of 'initiatives' in the present section is based on the Government of India's best-practice-compendium. *See* GOI, Department of Administrative Reforms and Public Grievances, *Initiatives and Best Practices of Government of India for Effective and Responsive Administration,* New Delhi, November 1997.

2

Application of New Public Management in Local Government

ASHOK SHARMA

The twenty-first century is witnessing radical change in the nature and role of public administration. The classical public administration, based on Taylor's Scientific Management and the Weberian model of bureaucracy do not seem to fulfil the desired expectations of a changing society. The development of New Public Administration (NPA) and Development Administration has given a new orientation to public administration. It has resulted in significant changes and improvement in managing public organizations. The propounders of the concept of Reinventing Government have motivated the scholars of public administration all over the world to have a relook and then reassess the present system of the machinery of government which, by and large, has failed to invoke optimum people's participation in the governance process and provide social justice to all the sections of society.

The traditional model of Public Administration has passed through a turbulent phase. Bloated and inefficient bureaucracy, alienation of the citizenry from administration and resource crunch faced on sustained basis has further sharpened inadequacies of traditional model to deliver goods. The social science literature in general and Public Administration,

Economics, Political Science and Management literature in particular has come up with alternative models of Public Administration and the New Public Management (NPM) has emerged as one of the leading models in that series.[1]

David Osborne and Ted Gaebler[2] had listed ten principles of Reinventing Government which later on became the sound base of NPM. The principles are:

1. Catalytic Government: Steering Rather Than Rowing.
2. Community-Owned Government: Empowering Rather Than Serving.
3. Competitive Government: Injecting Competition into Service Delivery.
4. Mission-Driven Government: Transforming Rule-Driven Organizations.
5. Results-Oriented Government: Funding Outcomes, Not Inputs.
6. Customer-Driven Government: Meeting the Needs of the Customer, Not the Bureaucracy.
7. Enterprising Government: Earning Rather Than Spending.
8. Anticipatory Government: Prevention Rather Than Cure.
9. Decentralized Government: From Hierarchy to Participation and Teamwork.
10. Market-Oriented Government: Leveraging Change Through the Market.

Public Administration "constantly changes with changes in the philosophy of state, objectives of governments and values of people. It is a dynamic apparatus of State, not a static instrument".[3] The new model of administrative system which is known as NPM provides foundations to the concept of good governance and has aimed at entrepreneurial role of public organizations with a market-based public administration resulting in effectiveness and economy in the functioning of public organizations.[4]

Many countries are trying to operationalize the concept of NPM and have started structural adjustments and new type of state intervention to seek cooperation and help from community organizations and citizens. Some have also tried to limit the role of the state including attempts made at downsizing of bureaucracy, devolution of authority, cost-reduction, contracting out certain operative functions, developing a result-oriented appraisal system and adopting a market-orientation of governmental activities. This has been supplemented by ensuring accountability through an effective operating system. The administration is thus moving from rule to result-orientation, from system to enterprise, obedience to reward, inaction to action, centralization to decentralization and from the duties of administration to the rights of citizens.[5]

NPM in Local Government

Let us discuss certain aspects of NPM in relation to the system of local government in India:

More Decentralisation in the Working of Local Government

Until recently, in most administrative organizations, including the local government agencies, powers have remained, by and large, centralized, but due to advancement in the field of technology and communication this situation is changing. It is a truism that a system of democratic form of government for its success requires local self-governing institutions.[6] Now, local government institutions throughout the world, are trying to decentralize their services to satisfy public demands and needs. It is believed that the decentralized institutions are more flexible than the centralized institutions and they can respond quickly to changing circumstances and customers' needs. Secondly, decentralized institution are considered more effective than the centralized ones, since the serving points in the former are available closer to the users of services provided by these institutions. Thirdly, decentralized institutions are more innovative. They know where the shoe is really pinching. Hence, they try to outline a sound blue-print of the services to be provided to their citizens. Fourthly, decentralized institutions trigger higher morale, greater commitment and enhanced productivity among the personnel working in them.

The local government institutions in India, therefore, should try to further decentralize their organizational structures. In most metropolitan towns, municipal institutions are formally decentralized in zones but the necessary infrastructure, adequate personnel and other required resources are not being provided to them. Therefore, these decentralized outposts of municipal institutions are not delivering satisfactory goods to the citizens. Decentralized government is one of the important principles identified by Osborne and Gaebler in *"Reinventing Government"* and if the NPM is to be properly adopted, the local government institutions and their present structure has to be decentralized and many more small municipal zones within the framework of the present municipal corporations and councils need to be created so that the decentralized units may be able to serve the local population more efficiently and effectively.

Making Local Administration Accountable, Transparent and Efficient through E-Governance

In the contemporary information era, e-governance has become an essential feature of local governance. It is a pre-condition to good and transparent administration. With e-democracy, backed by e-government and e-business acting as the prime mover for economic growth, a new combination of forces is emerging on the scene.

In order to become a part of the developed global community, good governance through e-governance is a necessity for the developmental process. Emphasizing on participatory, transparent and accountable administration, it undertakes responsibility for allocation of resources to the poorest and the most-vulnerable sections of society.

In most local governments institutions, the local bureaucracy is alleged to be insensitive to public concerns. It is in a habit of delaying work and seek something extra for making things move. Normally the citizens do not complain against this situation and feel helpless. This state of affairs must change.

IT can make a material difference to the speed of information and the quality of decisions. The areas where IT can successfully be applied are:

(a) Authentication of Statements
(b) Access to Public Documents
(c) Online Payments
(d) Filing of Returns
(e) Complaints, Grievances and Suggestions
(f) Partnering with Government
(g) Online Delivery of Services

An example of how IT affects human lives and can help local governments perform better is a project called *Sankaryam*[7] (meaning facility) which is developed by Visakhapatnam Municipal Corporation (VMC).

Visakhapatnam Municipal Corporation went about the task of onlining all its civic services. These include:

(i) Online payment of municipal dues
(ii) Online registration of births and deaths
(iii) Instant issuance of birth and death certificates
(iv) Online filing and settlement of complaints and grievances
(v) Online tracking of garbage lifting
(vi) Online tracking of building plan status
(vii) Online infrastructural works for better control over expenditure

Local government institutions throughout the country should learn lessons from the experience of Vishakhapatnam Municipal Corporations to improve their working.

Citizen's Charter of Urban Local Bodies

Citizen's Charter is a commitment of local bodies to provide all residents of their respective area in the realm of following services.

(a) Proper roads and drains.
(b) Adequate and safe drinking water.
(c) Effective sanitary arrangements.
(d) Appropriate street lighting.
(e) Prompt registration of births and deaths.
(f) Sufficient number of parks .

Commitment to Municipal Institutions under the Citizen's Charter

Municipalities and municipal corporations are expected to carry out the functions and duties with objectivity and transparency, promptness and efficiency, commitment for quality and standard of service, courtesy and helpfulness and Leaflets will be provided about the procedure to be followed for obtaining various permissions/certificates.

These values are incorporated in the monographs and brochures published by the local government institutions, urban as well rural, in their citizen's characters. In fact, all local bodies should try to develop their citizen's charters which, in turn, can become documents of expectations of the citizens and their fulfillment by these bodies. In this respect an example of service centers opened by municipal corporations in Andhra Pradesh can become a motivating example for other local bodies to follow.

Service Centres

Service centers have been opened in all municipalities and municipal corporations in Andhra Pradesh with effect from 14th May, 2001 to receive applications and dispose them of in a time-bound manner as shown in Table 1:

Table 1: Time Frame for Disposal of Cases in Service Centres

Sl. No.	*Activity*	*Time Schedule*
1.	Assessment of Property tax and allocation of door No.	15 days
2.	Disposal of Building Applications	15 days
3.	Sanction of Water Supply House Service connection (a) General category (b) OYT	30 days 10 days
4.	Issuance of Birth and Deaths certificates	5 days

Mechanism for Implementation

Every citizen who wishes to avail of the above mentioned services has to submit an application at the Service Centre duly enclosing the required documents between 10.30 am and 1.30 pm on a working day. The Assistant incharge of the Service Centre gives an acknowledgement to the applicant indicating the date and time on which he can obtain permission/certificate from the Service Centre as per the time frame indicated above. Prepared permission letters/certificates are issued from the Service Centre between 2.00 pm to 5.00 pm.

Payment of Compensation to the Applicants

To ensure the adherence of time schedule in providing the above services, ULBs were directed to pay a compensation of Rs. 50 per day to an applicant if the time schedule was not followed in accordance with the declared policy. This amount has to be collected by ULBs from the persons responsible for the delay in rendering the service. This step will definitely go a long way in tightening the time management systems of local bodies.

Grievance Redressal

Public grievances relating to the services are redressed as shown in Table 2.

Table 2: Time Frame for Redressal of Grievances

Sl. No.	*Item of work*	*Time frame*
1.	Garbage clearance	1 day
2.	Clearing of drains	2 days
3.	Anti larval operations	Once in two weeks
4.	Provision of dust bins	2 weeks
5.	Repairs to pipe line leakages	1 day
6.	Replacement of Street lights	5 days
7.	Repairs to road cuttings	7 days

Every local government agency expects from its citizens:

(a) to help city administration in rendering services in an efficient manner;
(b) to be prompt in payment of property tax, water charges, trade license fee;
(c) to use dust-bins for depositing garbage and not to throw it in drains;
(d) to use drinking water without any wastage;
(e) to avoid open defecation;
(f) to construct buildings as per approved layouts and plans; and
(g) to avoid un-authorized constructions and deviations to sanctioned plans.

Customer Driven Government at Local Level

There are number of ways to listen to the voice of the citizen at the local level government. "Supported by vibrant local institutions, the people at large achieve a new identity that moves the government-citizen relationship into a bilateral mould".[8] A few local governments survey their customers six months or every year to see whether the service actually yielded the desired results. For instance, Delhi, Mumbai, Chennai etc. survey their residents to see what they like and dislike about their city and government. Further, several housing authorities and other development authorities use resident councils to be in touch with their customers. The Delhi Development Authority (DDA), Jaipur Municipal Corporation (JMC) etc. use customer council to get feedback, particularly on new ideas.

Some cities have systems that track responses to inquiries and complaints, to reduce their response time. Ahmedabad is one such city.

Enterprising Government at Local Level

Making profits through development deals is one of the more aggressive methods used by enterprising governments.[9] Perhaps the safest way to raise non-tax revenue is simply to charge fees to those who use public services. User fees have become ever more popular as the resistance to tax increases has mounted. A few local governments generate 30 percent of their operating budgets from fees and another five percent from concessions. The average local government raises more than 25 percent of its revenue from user fees for water and sewer services, garbage collection, health services, recreation facilities, building inspections, and parking.

The most common form a necessity takes in local government is fiscal crisis, but economic crises, political crises, and even natural crises such as earthquakes and flood can create demands for change. Fundamental changes are difficult and painful, fraught with uncertainty and risk. Most local government that embark on the journey need outside help—from foundations, consultants, civic organizations. Some local governments—Delhi, Mumbai, Ludhiana, etc.—are instrumental in creating change, whether through their expertise; their financial resources; or their political activism.

The Entrepreneurial Revolution in Local Government

In our observation of local government, we have discerned a

number of factors supportive of fundamental change. Cities with healthy civic infrastructures are those in which citizens, community based organizations (CBOs), NGOs, business and media outlets are committed to public welfare. Local governments—such as Delhi, Mumbai, Visakhapatnam etc—that enjoy such commitment find it much easier to make fundamental changes.

It is not enough that a leader has a vision of change; he must get other community leaders to buy into that vision. "The key element is a collective vision of a city future—a sense of where it's headed."[10] A shared vision is not the same thing as a consensus. Entrepreneurial leaders in local government, i.e. Mayor/Chairman, rally their communities to their visions, rather than accepting a least common denominator consensus.

REFERENCES

1. Ghuman, B.S. New Public Management: Theory and Practice, "*Indian Journal of Public Administration*" XL VII (Oct.-Dec. 2001) pp. 778-79.
2. David Osborne and Ted Gaebler, *Reinventing Government: How the Entrepreneurial Spirit is Transforming the Public Sector?* (Reading—Addison Wesley, 1992).
3. Ali, Sofi and Rao, Anita, "Reinventing Public Administration for 21st Century" *Indian Journal of Public Administration* XL VI (April-June 2000) p. 169.
4. Hood, Christopher, "A Public Manager for All Reasons", *Public Administration,* Vol. 69, 1991.
5. Jan-Eric-Lane, *The Public Sector: Concept, Models and Approaches,* (New Delhi, 1995), pp. 60-63.
6. Singh, Mohinder, Democratic Decentralisation in India After 73rd Amendment: Some Issues and Challenges" in Shiv Raj Singh, and others (edn.). *Public Administration in the New Millennium-Challenges and Prospects.* New Delhi: Anamika Publishers 2003, p. 67
7. Jaju, Sanjay, "Information Technology & Governance", paper presented at the National Seminar on "Municipal Administration

in India—changing Scenario" held by the Department of Public Administration, University of Rajasthan, Jaipur during 15-17 March, 2002.

8. 'Sharma, Arvind K., "Administrative Reforms in India During 1990s" in Shiv Raj Singh, *et al.*, eds, p. 431.
9. David Osborne and Ted Gaebler, *op. cit.*
10. David Osborne and Ted Gaebler, *op. cit.*

3

Applicability and Sustainability of New Public Management

INDERJEET SINGH SODHI

We find that "Through the ages and across the territorial frontiers, one constant factor in the field of Public Administration is the quest for change. Reinvention has served as a vehicle for harmonising and ventilating ideas and suggestions from various quarters about how Public Administration should be reformed"[1]. The traditional model of public administration was based on structure and process of outcomes, tended to be stubborn, rule oriented and bureaucratic. Patrick Dunleavy observed, "During the 1970s, conventional public administration approaches began to look tired and undynamic. By contrast, political economy offered a logical deductive model of how government agencies behave, with clear directions for policy analysis and simple normative recommendations for reform, public choice accounts became widely accepted because they fitted closely with everyday or common-sense views of bureaucracy."[2]

In late 1980s and early 1990s, in UK and some other European countries, the administrative hierarchical bureaucratic model was being denounced and replaced by new managerial approach[3]. New Public Management (NPM) emerged in the beginning of the 1990s in response to the challenges of technological change, rigidity, international competitiveness, strictly hierarchical model of bureaucracy, and globalization. New Public Management is known by reinventing Government, minimal government, market based Public Administration or Managerialism.

The NPM has seen its expansion and diversification in a number of developed and developing countries. "The emergence of a post-industrial, knowledge-based, global economy has undermined old realities throughout the world and has created enormous opportunities for governments at all levels to respond effectively to these realities."[4] Many of the change programmes within UK public services in the 1980s and 1990s fell under the NPM umbrella as they included a simultaneous growth of marketisation and managerlisation. "Gradually a series of reforms under the garb of New Public Management were introduced globally, towards bringing about sweeping changes in the government system, institutions and functioning."[5]

According to Osborne and Gaebler[6], "The kind of governments that developed during the industrial area, with their sluggish, centralised bureaucracies, their pre-occupation with rules and regulations, and their hierarchical chains of commands, no longer work very well" (1992, 11-12). In fact, while they served their earlier purposes, "bureaucratic institutions...increasingly fail us"(15).

NPM is a concern[7] with the ability of public administration to secure the economic, efficient and effective provision of public services (Hughes 1999), and a concern for the excesses of professional power within public services and the consequent disempowerment of service users (Falconer and Ross 1999). The traditional institutions, systems and processes are becoming more marginal. New processes and institutions, including NGOs and CBOs, are becoming more central to public policy. A government could fundamentally transform their organisations and systems to dramatically increase their economy, efficiency, effectiveness, capacity, and adaptability to innovate.

The field of public administration has "a long history of popular reform movements". Many of these reforms have failed to deliver the improvements promised. The current 'reinventing government' reforms, which follow largely from the writings of David Osborne and his co-authors, claim to establish a new governmental paradigm based on liberating employers and citizens to do their best and using new management methods to get the most out of what government does."[8]

Doctrines of New Public Management

Since the emergence of NPM model, there has been some debate over the precise nature of the NPM (Dunleavy and Hood 1994; Plynn: chapter 4, in Kate McLaughlin, Stephen P. Osborne and Ewan Ferlie eds., 2002, Hood 1991). NPM comprised following eight doctrines:

(i) The promotion of discipline and parsimony in resource allocation (Metcalfe and Richards 1990);

(ii) A stress on private sector style of management and their superiority (Wilcox and Harrow 1992);

(iii) A focus on entrepreneurial management, as opposed to the traditional bureaucratic focus of the public administrator (Clarke and Newman 1993);

(iv) Explicit standards and measures of performance (Osborne *et al.*, 1995);

(v) A shift to the promotion of competition in the provision of public services (Walsh 1995);

(vi) Separation of political decision-making from the direct management of public services (Stewart 1996);

(vii) The importance of the disaggregation and decentralisation of public services (Pollit *et al.* 1998); and

(viii) An emphasis on output controls (Boyne 1999).

Characteristics of New Public Management

The NPM is an expanded view of reinventing government, which began in the 1980s almost entirely at the local level[9]. The Denhardts argue that the new public management, which incorporates reinvention, is a "a cluster of ideas and practices...that seeks, at their core, to use their private sector and business approaches in the public sector."[10] The characteristics of NPM, according to Sandford Borins[11], are:

(i) Providing high-quality services that citizens value;
(ii) Demanding, measuring, and rewarding improved organisational and individual performance;
(iii) Advocating managerial autonomy, particularly by reducing central agency controls;
(iv) Recognising the importance of providing the human and technological resources managers need to meet their performance targets; and
(v) Maintaining receptiveness to competition and open-mindedness about which public purposes should be performed by public servants as opposed to the private sector or non-governmental organisations.

Applicability of New Public Management

The traditional public administration, despite its many important contributions, has come to be seen as synonymous with control, bureaucracy, and hierarchy. NPM is an alternative of formal bureaucracies plagued with excessive rules, preoccupied with control, and bound by rigid budgeting and personnel systems. NPM carded with it a new set of values, specifically a set of values largely drawn from the private sector and is concerned with the implementation of new techniques.

The new public management is composed of the following ideas:

(a) Government should improve the quality of its service;

(b) Government should be result oriented;
(c) Government should be customer driven;
(d) Government should be entrepreneurial;
(e) Government should improve its accountability to the public interest;
(f) Government should improve objectives and measure performance;
(g) Government should improve the quality of regulation;
(h) Government should ensure accountability and performance of administrator;
(i) Government should provide more flexibility to the civil servants; and
(j) Government should devolve more and more authority.

NPM has been portrayed as a global paradigm emerging in response to economic, institutional, political and ideological changes (Box *et al*, 2001); Kamensky 1996, Kettl, 1997; Osborne and Gaebler 1992; OECD 1995). Over the two decades, the NPM movement has literally swept the world—developed and developing. During this period, the public managers have sought to—

(i) Decentralise decision making;
(ii) Restructure bureaucratic agencies;
(iii) Streamline agency processes;
(iv) Redefine organisational missions;
(v) Privatise functions previously provided by government;
(vi) Find new innovative ways to achieve results;
(vii) Concentrate on accountability and high performance;
(viii) Establish new processes for measuring productivity and effectiveness; and
(ix) Reflect a strengthened commitment to accountability.

The revolution of NPM movement has increased pressure on state bureaucracies to become more responsive to citizens as clients. "The New Public Management has championed a vision of public managers as the entrepreneurs of a new, leaner, and increasingly privatised government, emulating not only the practices but also the values of business. Proponents of the New Public Management have developed their arguments largely through contrasts with the old public administration."[12]

Sustainability of NPM

We know that "there is a long standing tradition in public administration" supporting the idea that "government should be run like a business." For the most part, this recommendation has meant that government agencies should adopt practices, ranging from 'scientific management' to 'total quality management', that have been found useful in the private sector. The New Public Management takes this idea one step further, arguing that government should not only adopt the techniques of business administration, but should adopt certain business values as well. The New Public Management thus becomes a normative model for public administration and public management.[13]

NPM represents a style of management that is much closer to the government's emphasis on, and desire to encourage:

- (i) Social entrepreneurship.
- (ii) Economic entrepreneurship.
- (iii) Political entrepreneurship.
- (iv) Administrative entrepreneurship.
- (v) Market entrepreneurship.

The NPM has—

- (i) helped to address fundamental weaknesses in the management of public sector.
- (ii) helped to address fundamental weaknesses in the systems of accountability and control in public services.
- (iii) brought benefits of service effectiveness to service sector.

(iv) brought benefits of cost efficiency in the public management.

Some thinkers like Terry (1993, 1998) have suggested that public entrepreneurship threaten to undermine democratic and constitutional values such as fairness, justice, representation, and participation.

Regarding the sustainability of NPM, questions are raised on—

(i) about the inherent contradictions in the movement (Fox, 1996);
(ii) the values promoted by it (Celeon and Denhardt 2000, Frederickson 1996; Schachter 1997)];
(iii) the tensions between the emphasis on decentralisation promoted in the marketmodel, the need for coordination in the public sector (Peters and Savoi 1996) ;
(iv) the implied roles and relationships of the executive and legislative branches (Carroll and Lynn 1996); and
(v) the implications of the privatisation movement for democratic values and the public interest (McCabe and Vinzant 1999).

The pragmatic new regime is attempting to sue a wide variety of policy instruments. The reforms are concerned with creating an entrepreneurial and user oriented culture within public organisations. The NPM is a paradigm which is likely to continue as a dominant mode of organisation. It has been broadened from the earlier narrow concern with marketisation to one which focusses upon governance as the pre-eminent task of public management.

Theoretically, the NPM is a sustainable paradigm for the organisation and management of civil services which can survive:

(i) The challenges, from time to time, posed to it.
(ii) The shift of political control at the central/state level.

(iii) The sudden shift in the policy.
(iv) The major onslaught of the world economy.
(v) The threats put forward by the terrorists.
(vi) The restrictions imposed by the trade policy.

The civil services are undergoing an archetype shift from a previously dominant public administration archetype to a novel NPM archetype[14]. The coherent attempts and sustained energy will be needed to move on to a novel template that goes beyond the NPM. In a Seminal article defining the new public management, Hood[15] (1991) notes that its emphasis on the values of economy and parsimony could come at the cost of the ethical values of honesty and fairness and the organisational values of robustness and resilience.

Regarding the sustainability of NPM model we have to see "the extent to which it has sufficient conceptual coherence to provide an alternative to public administration as either a theoretical construct for academic research or an approach to the management of public services."[16] Questions and debate are arising whether the NPM is a direct competitor for public administration, as a new, converged, paradigm of public management[17] or it is instead a development within the continuing, and nationally divergent, paradigm of public administration[18]. It is not a static phenomenon rather a dynamic and evolving one.

NPM emphasised that "the primary role of the public servant is to help citizens articulate and meet their shared interest rather than to attempt to control or steer society."[19] It is not a static phenomenon rather a dynamic and an evolving one. Indian model of public management reform emphasizes a continuing strong role for government and maintains a career public service working in the traditional and modern departmental structures. The main task of the government becomes the management of the complex network of public service provision. The NPM be modified into a more public interest intensive approach.

Public administrators should "focus on their responsibility to serve and empower citizens as they manage public organisations and implement public policy. In other words, with citizens at the forefront, the emphasis should not be placed on either steering or rowing the governmental boat, but rather on building public institutions marked by integrity and responsiveness"[20].

NOTES

1. Sofi Ali and Anita Rao, "Reinventing Public Administration for 21st" Century" in Indian Journal of Public Administration (IJPA), Vol. XLVI, No. 2, April-June 2000, p. 186.
2. Patrick Dunleavy, *Democracy, Bureaucracy and Public Choice: Economic Explanations in Political Science.* London: Harvester, Wheatsheaf, 1991, p. 147.
3.
4. Ramesh K. Arora, "Introduction: Public Administration: Resilience and Rejuvenation" in Ramesh K. Arora (Eds.), *Public Administration—Fresh Perspectives,* Aalekh Publishers, Jaipur, 2004, p. 11.
5. Uma Medury, "Reinventing Public Administration: The New Public Management Perspective" in Ramesh K. Arora (Eds.), *op. cit.*, p. 87.
6. David Osborne and Ted Gaebler, *Reinventing Government: How the Entrepreneurial Spirit is Transforming the Public Sector,* Reading-Addison Wesley, 1992.
7. Kate McLaughlin, Stephen P. Osporne and Edwan Ferlie (Eds.), *New Public Management—Current Trends and Future Prospects,* Routledge, London, 2002, p. 9.
8. Daniel W. Williams, Reinventing the Proverbs of Government" in *Public Administration Review* (PAR), Vol. 60. No. 6. Nov.-Dec. 2002, p. 522.
9. Paul Tasks and Mark Schneider, "The Bureaucratic Entrepreneur: The Case of City Manager", *Public Administration Review* 54 (July/ August 1994), pp. 336-340.
10. Robert, B. Denhardt and Janet Vinzant Denhardt, "The New Public Service: Serving Rather than Steering", in *Public Administration Review 60,* Nov.-Dec. 2000.
11. Sandfor Borins (1995), Summary: Government in Transition—A

New Paradigm in New Pub. Admn. in Commonwealth Secretariat, ed. *Government in Transition: The Inaugural Conference of the Commonwealth Association for Pub. Admn. and Management* (Toronto: Commonwealth Secretariat): 5-11.

12. Robert B. Denhardt and Janet Vinzant Denhardt, *op. cit.*, p. 549.
13. RobertB. Denhardt and Janet Vinzant Denhardt, *op. cit.*, p. 541.
14. Kate McLaughlin, Stephen P. Osborne and Ewan Ferlie, *op. cit.*, pp. 352-53.
15. Hood, Christopher, 1991. A Public Management for all Seasons? *Public Administration* 69 (I): 3-19.
16. Stephen P. Osborne and Kate McLaughlin, "The New Public Management in Context" in Kate McLaughlin. *et al.*, *op. cit.*, p. 11.
17. Gow, J. and Dufour, C.(2000) Is the new public management a paradigm? Does it matter? *International Review of Administrative Sciences* (66, 4) pp. 573-598.
18. Lynn, L.(1998) The New Public Management as an international phenomenon: a skeptical viewpoint in L. Janes and K. Schedler (Eds.) *International Perspectives on the New Public Management* (JAI Press, Greenwich, CT).
19. Robert B. Denhardt and Janet Vinzant Denhardt, *op. cit.*, p. 549.
20. Robert B. Denhardt and Janet Vinzant Denhardt, op. cit., p. 549.

REFERENCES

Boyne, G. (1999) Processes, "Performance and Best value in local government" *Local Government Studies* (25, 3), pp. 1-15.

Caroll, James, and Dahlia Bradshow Lynn (1996). The Future of Federal Reinvention: Congressional Perspectives, *Public Administration Review* 56(3): 299-304.

Clarke, M. and Navman, J. (1993), The right to manage: a second managerial resolution?

Dehelon, Linda and Robert B. Denhardt (2000), The Political Theory of Reinvention, *Public Administration Review* 60(2): 89-97.

Dunleavy, P. and Hood. C. (1994), "From Old Public Administration to New Public Management" in *Public Money and Management,* July-September.

Fox, Charles (1996), Reinventing Government as Postmodern Symbolic Politics. *Public Administration Review* 56(3): 256-61.

Frederickson, H. George (1996), "Comparing Reinventing

Government Movement with the New Public Administration" in *Public Administration Review* 60(2): 89-97.

Hood, Christopher (1991), "A Public Management for All Seasons?" *Public Administration,* 69: 3-19.

Kettl, Donald F. (1997), "The Global Revolution in Public Management: Driving Themes, Missing Link", *Journal of Policy Analysis and Management,* 16: 446-462.

McCabe, Barbara, and Janet Vinzant (1999), Governance Lessons: The Case of Charter Schools. *Administration and Society* 31(3); 361-77.

Metcalfe, L. and Richards, S. (1990), *Improving Public Service Management,* Sage, London. The right to manage: a second managerial revolution?

OECD (1995), *Governance in Transition: Public Management Reforms in OECD Countries,* Paris, PUMA/OECD.

Osborne, S. Bovaird, T., Martin, J. Tricker, M. and Waterson, P. (1995), Performance Management and Accountability in Complex Programmes. Finance Accountability and Management (11, 1) pp. 1-18

Peters, B. Guy, and Donald Savoie (1996), Managing in Coherence: The Coordination and Empowerment Conundrum. *Public Administration Review* 56(3). 281-9.

Politt, C. Birchell, J. and Putnam, K. (1998), *Decentralising Public Service Management* (Macmillan, London).

Schachter, Hindy Lauer (1997), *Reinventing Government or Reiventing Ourselves.* Albony. NY: State University of New York Press.

Terry, Larry D. (1993), Why we should Abandon the Misconceived Quest to Reconcilc Public Entrepreneurship with Democracy. *Public Administration Review* 53(4): 393-5

Terry, Larry D. (1998), "Administrative Leadership, Neo-Managerialism, and the Public Management Movement" in *Public Administration Review* 58(3): 194-200.

Walsh, K. (1995), *Public Services and Market Mechanism: Competition, Contracting and the New Public Management* (Macmillan, London).

Stewart, J. (1996), A Dogma of our Times: Separating Policy Making from Implementation. *Public Money and Management,* July-September.

Willcox, L. and Harrow, J. (eds) (1992), *Rediscovering Public Service Management* (McGraw Hill, London).

4

New Public Management

NOORJAHAN BAVA

The intellectual field of Public Administration rooted in the parent disciplines of political science and public law has witnessed during its long chequered history spanning over a century many approaches, theories, trends and paradigms. The latest addition to its tool-kit is what has come to be known as the New Public Management (NPM). Ever since the 1980s New Public Management has emerged as the new paradigm in the theory and practice of public administration.

Movement Towards Public Management

It must be noted that the emergence of the new public management paradigm in the 1980s was preceded by the public management approach since the 1970s. Public Management approach originated as a result of two developments—the launching of the Implementation Movement[1] by Jeffrey Pressman and Aaron Wildavsky in 1973 and the holding of two National Conferences on Public Management, the first in 1991 at Syracuse University and the second one in 1993, which led to the publication of two great volumes on Public Management[2]. These two thinkers gave a clarion call to public administrationists to focus on implementation of public programmes for good results—a call to move away from their conventional focus on organisational structures and processes to public programmes and the results they produced. The implementation movement thus brought the issues of implementation and performance to the centre-stage of the debate for the first time. As a result implementation studies moved beyond a base in public administration and even beyond political science to a far broader, more interdisciplinary foundation. This is because the organisational-structural-process focus of traditional public administration left important issues unanswered. From these two trends was born the new field of public management.

On one level the difference between public administration and public management was 'cosmetic'. Some scholars embraced public management because it had a "livelier feel and represented fresh thinking". Others sought in public management a far more positive view of government and its programmes. The practitioners of the new public policy programme firmly believed that good managers, if properly trained, could make the difference between success and failures. In seeking to build success instead of understanding failure, the practitioners rejected the implementation movement. And in focusing on what managers could do instead of how organizations behaved, they rejected public administration (Kettl, p. 5)[3].

However, both implementation movement and traditional public administration contributed to the new debate on public management. Implementation established the importance of programme as a fundamental unit of analysis. Public administration argued the need for a solid budgetary process, right human resources system, and functional organizations. But in their headlong rush to build something new, some public management scholars have glossed over the critical building blocks that public administrationists lovingly laboured so long to build and that which implementation students in a short time had created (Kettl, p. 5).

Nevertheless, it was impossible to ignore that in public management something very new was sweeping the study of governance and public policy. Public management grew haphazardly and in some cases it ignored long established truths and in other cases by importing fresh disciplinary ideas by the truckload. It became an interdisciplinary approach. However, public management is neither traditional public administration nor policy analysis. It borrows from a host of disciplines and many different methodological approaches. While Graham, Cole and Hays see public management as a branch of the larger field of public administration or public affairs, others argue that it is a technical sub-field of public administration.[4]

Public administration, writes Owen E. Hughes, "is an activity serving the public, and public servants carry out policies derived from others. It is concerned with procedures, with translating policies into action and with office management. Public management does include administration, but also involves organization to achieve objectives with maximum efficiency, as well as genuine responsibility for results. These two elements were not necessarily present in the traditional administrative system. Public administration focuses on process, on procedures and propriety, while public management involves much more. Instead of merely following instructions, a public manager focuses on achieving results and taking responsibility for doing so" (pp. 5-6)[5].

There has been a trend towards the use of the words 'management and manager' has become sharper. Public administration is clearly losing favour as a description of the work carried out by the public servants. Usage of the term 'manager' is becoming more common where once 'administrator' was used (Pollitt 1990)[6]. Usage of the term public management is gaining ground, while public administration now seems old-fashioned, if not obsolete.

The switch over to 'management' focus implied the concern for 'strategy' and 'external environment', which was different from the 'internal' concerns of public administration. As Rainey (1990) argues: public administration literature has been "information rich and skill poor, too broadly discursive and philosophical and too preoccupied with general ethical and normative issues to provide guidelines for managers of public organizations"[7].

Genesis of New Public Management (NPM)

The rise of NPM has been a function of a host of factors political, ideological, technological, national, international, global and intellectual. As Christopher Hood observes:[8]

"The rise of new public management over the past 15 years is one of the most striking international trends in public administration...NPM is emphatically not a uniquely British development. NPM's rise is linked with four other administrative mega trends namely:

(i) attempts to slow down or reverse government growth in terms of overt public spending and staffing;
(ii) the shift towards privatisation and quasi-privatisation;
(iii) the development of automation, particularly information technology, in the production and distribution of public services; ands
(iv) the development of a more international agenda, increasingly focused on general issues of public management, policy design, decision styles and intergovernmental cooperation".

Political Factors

These include political regime changes in UK, USA, Thatcherism (1979-1997), Reaganomics (1980-84) and OECD countries ushering in conservative party governments and the pursuit of policies of privatisation and marketization leading to blistering attacks on the scope, size and methods of the public sector, the 'Welfare State', 'the Administrative State', and failure and inherent inability of the public bureaucracy to provide economic, efficient and effective public services.

Ideological

The rise of New Right ideologies-neo-classical economics such as Public Choice, Transactions Cost and Principal-Agent Theories contained in the writings of Vincent Ostrom[9], Niskanen[10], Buchanan[11], Tullock[12], and others.

Intellectual

(i) David Osborne and Tedd Gaebler's book entitled Reinventing Government (1992)[13].
(ii) National Performance Report (1993) containing 800 recommendations launched by the then U.S. Vice-President Al-Gore during the Clinton Administration for establishing 'entrepreneurial' government.
(iii) Rise of Managerialism: And rise of Managerialism with its emphasis on the functions of strategy, managing internal component and managing external environment, Allison (1982)[14].

Technological Changes

Technological change is proliferating interrelationships and making them achievable particularly in electronics and information technology. The development of new technologies enables activities to be shared across business units. The growing sophistication of information systems may also act to open up possibilities for interrelationships (Bowman *et al.*, 1987, p. 52)[15].

Global forces affect the public sector as much as the private sector. Technological change makes it possible to introduce new management systems into government. Information and data of all kinds can be gathered and transmitted cheaply, and transformed into performance information, which, in turn, allows management to be decentralised. By itself this could lead to substantial management change in government, compared to the primitive technological base of the traditional model of administration. Besides, the 'interrelationships' arising from technological change could lead to better communication within the organization and competition or joint ventures with the private sector. These points are already occurring in the public sector.

Globalization and Competitiveness

Economic forces—Globalisation and Competitiveness constituted further imperative for public sector change. It gave rise to the realisation that the management and efficiency of the public sector affects the private economy and national competitiveness. The OECD claims "all governments of member countries now recognise and accept that improving public management is an integral part of the structural adjustments needed for better economic performance in a changing global environment (OECD, 1990, p. 1)[16].

The trend towards globalisation also affects the management of the public sector. With the spread of new ideas and the impact of technological changes, national barriers are becoming increasingly artificial. Also, in a world of economic competition, the role of governments can be an important factor in creating 'competitive advantage'. Government policy does affect national advantage, both positively and negatively (Porter, 1990, p. 617)[17].

The OECD argues that competitiveness of an economy is affected by the health, education and training of its workforce, the efficiency of its tax administration or the encouragement of small enterprise development and these are provided by public services in most countries (OECD, 1990a, p. 4)[18]. Globalization, therefore, adds an extra imperative to the reform of administrative structures.

Given the government's role in assisting national competitiveness and the move to globalisation, there was some concern with the competence of the government. It is not just the Americans who worry about the competence in an era of economic change and economic uncertainties. The traditional model of administration may not have provided 'the competence' required for challenging times (Owen, p. 19). This model of administration may need to change towards 'a more subtle, and thoughtful role for policy-makers' through changes from bureaucratic forms of public administration to "more flexible structures" (Porter, 1990, p. 617)[19].

Changes in the private sector led directly to change in the public sector with new public management being implemented in many countries. There was similarity in the direction of the managerial reform agenda of many countries. There has been "structural reorganisation aimed at improving the coordination and implementation of policy.... Much emphasis continues to be placed in all (OECD) countries on improving the management of human resources and on realigning financial management systems to focus more on the results and outputs of government activities, and on how these may best be measured" (OECD, 1991b, p. 7)[20].

Downsizing the Bureaucracy

Because of the ideological, theoretical and global challenges, governments have begun probably the greatest transformation in their public services. There have been two different changes. First, there is a trend towards the 'marketisation' of the public sector, to shift public activities to the private sector through contracting out of activities and other ways. Secondly, there is the trend away from bureaucracy as an organising principle within the public sector. The two are, of course, related, in that one reason for marketisation is the presumed failure of bureaucracy, and provision of public service by markets is the main avenue pursued as an alternative to bureaucracy. These are manifestations of the New Right ideology. As Pollitt argues "managerialism is the acceptable face of new right thinking concerning the state. For new-right believers, better management provides a label under which private sector disciplines can be introduced into the public services, political control can be strengthened, budget trimmed, professional autonomy reduced, public service unions weakened and a quasi-competitive framework erected to flush out the 'natural' inefficiencies of bureaucracy" (Pollitt, 1990, p. 49)[21].

Critique of the Traditional Model by New-Right Theorists

From the 1970s, the public services encountered increasing criticism in most developed countries. Critics identified three main problems. First, the model of political control was inadequate and illogical. Second, the theory of bureaucracy is no longer universally seen as providing technical efficiency as Weber thought it provided. Bureaucracy is also undemocratic. It may be ideal for control but not necessarily for management. Third, the public choice thinkers pointed out that bureaucracy took away the freedom of the individual and it was inefficient compared to the market.

The Problem of Political Control

The strict separation between politics and administration advocated by Wilson in the 1880s (which became one of the pillars of the traditional public administration and which was designed to counter the spoils system then still rife in the U.S., was never followed in its original home) was a myth. In reality, the relationship between government and administration far from being simple as the Wilson model suggests, is very complex and fluid, and does not reflect the formal, linear logic of the Wilson model. As Guy Peters (1989, p. 4) put it,[22]

"Administration and policy, instead of being discrete phenomena, are actually interrelated. The nature of the administrative system can influence the policy outputs of the political system in both an objective and subjective manner. Administration does make policy, although these policies are not always written and promulgated in the same manner as the rules made by legislatures and executives. Moreover, the operational rules developed by administrators can be more telling for the actual outcomes for individuals than are the formally promulgated rules".

The traditional form simply does not reflect the extensive, managerial and policy-making role performed by the modem public service. It imposes a negative form of control, which seeks to avoid embarrassing mistakes rather than provide any positive incentive to improve efficiency. The attempt to be 'non-political' meant reluctance to recognise the policy and political significance of public service work. Public servants also have an important managerial role, something more important than merely administering or following instructions.

The model of political control was unrealistic in that politics and administration are necessarily intertwined. The work of public servants is fundamentally political, though some attachment to the dichotomy still continues among practitioners (Rabin and Bowman, 1984, pp. 5-7)[23]. Though this theory was long considered unrealistic, it did form a major underpinning of the traditional model of public administration.

The Problem of Bureaucracy

The second problem with the traditional model is the Weberian model of bureaucracy. Critics argue that the structure and management of the traditional model were obsolete and in need of drastic reform. "Formal bureaucracy may have its advantages but also it breeds time-servers not innovators, makes them risk averse rather than risk-taking and waste resources instead of using them efficiently". Though it was an 'ideal type' for Weber, it is criticised for producing inertia, lack of enterprise, red-tape, mediocrity, inefficiency—all diseases thought to be endemic in public sector bodies. There are two particular problems with the theory of bureaucracy. First, "the relationship between bureaucracy and democracy" and, second, bureaucracy could no longer be considered as "a particularly efficient form of organization". With its formal rationality secrecy, rigidity and hierarchy there is bound to be conflict between bureaucracy and democracy. It is said that Weber 'described' bureaucracy rather than advocating it.

Weber noted, "every bureaucracy seeks to increase the superiority of the professionally informed by keeping their knowledge and instructions secret" adding that "the concept of the official secret is the specific invention of bureaucracy" (Gerth and Mills, 1970, p. 233). This concern still exists today as does the wider concern over the relationship between democracy and bureaucracy. This takes (impinges) the power of the citizen or the politician rendering political accountability problematic. In other words, it results in non-elected officials having wide powers over their lives.

The second problem of bureaucracy is the 'technical superiority'. The principle of hierarchy with its multiple levels and sub-levels of authority and with barriers that restricted progress beyond certain points, the principle of employment for life promotion based on seniority—all these features made the officials incompetent, inefficient and yet difficult to be removed from service. The system bred mediocrity not efficiency or excellence. The principle of political neutrality led in some cases to the idea of 'service to the nation', above and beyond that of giving advice to and carrying out the wishes of the elected government. This produced problems of accountability as the unelected officials acted as a sort of Mandarin class doing what they wanted instead of what the politicians wanted them to do.

The scathing attack on bureaucracy by behaviouralists focused on its tendency towards 'trained inefficiency', and 'goal-displacement' (Robert Merton, 1968, p. 260)[24]; bureaucrat's inability to learn from its errors (Michael Crozier 1964, p. 187)[25]; its 'input dominated structure' wherein output is only incidental; its indifference to and neglect of results; and its wrong assumption that results will flow naturally from organization.

The Public Choice Critique of Governmental Bureaucracy

Government bureaucracy greatly restricted the freedom of the individual and its power needed to be reduced in the name of 'choice'. Hayek (1944)[26] and Friedman (1980)[27] voiced the view that freedom was better than serfdom and consumer choice better than bureaucratic command. According to those market economists the bureaucratic structure did not provide an equivalent structure of incentives and rewards to those of the market.

Applying the rational choice assumptions of their theory the public choice thinkers criticised that bureaucrats will attempt to maximise their own utility, i.e., they aim to increase their own power, prestige and security, and income by using the hierarchical structure for their own ends instead of advancing the goals of the organization. From public choice perspective it is illogical to expect bureaucrats to be disinterested and motivated by higher ideals as Weber's model implies. According to them individual ambition can lead to outcome not necessarily in the best interest of the organization. Niskanen (1973, p. 23) argued that individual ambition leads to budget maximisation by the agency, because bureaucrats will benefit personally if they obtain a larger budget, as, this means they will have more staff, more power and a higher classification in the organization.

Ostrom sees bureaucracy as less efficient or effective than allowing choice through market competition, and consumer sovereignty and choice provide incentives to lower costs which are absent in the bureaucratic model of administration. Thus we see the 'Public Choice' arguments are directed towards reducing the government and reducing the bureaucracy. Their alternative is the market model.

New Public Management (NPM): Content

The 1980s and early 1990s witnessed the emergence of the New Public Management (NPM) approach in response to the inadequacies of the traditional model of administration. NPM takes many incarnations: 'managerialism' (Pollitt, 1990); 'new public management' (Hood, 1991); 'market-based public administration' (Lan and Rosenbloom, 1992)[28]; or 'entrepreneurial government' and 'Reinventing government' (Osborne and Gaebler, 1992). While NPM is used in pejorative sense by some, others contrast it with the earlier American usage of 'public management', which views it as a technical sub-field of public administration. Some view public management as a new way of looking at and carrying out management functions within the public sector. Others regard it as simply an uncritical adoption of the worst features of private management and ignoring the fundamental differences of the public sector environment. Managerialism is seen by some as against the traditions of the public service, inimical to service delivery and somehow undemocratic, with dubious theoretical backing. Critics from the public administration tradition argue that the good parts of the old model—high ethical standards, service to the state—are being cast aside in the headlong rush to adopt the new theory (Owen, p. 59).

Meaning and Nature of NPM

By whatever name it is known, NPM as a model represents a major shift from traditional public administration with its emphasis on the achievement of results and the personal responsibility of managers. There is a clear indication in NPM to move away from the classic rigid bureaucracy towards more flexible and flat forms of organization, personnel and financial management. NPM stands for organizational and personal objectives so as to enable the measurement of their achievement through performance indicators. The focus of the manager should change from process to result. It calls for systematic programme evaluations with a view to achieve the virtuous three E's: economy, efficiency and effectiveness (Pollitt, 1990, p. 59)[29]. NPM aims at reducing the economic role of the State/Government through privatization. It assigns the role of 'steering and not rowing' to the State, which has to be a facilitator and regulator rather than direct provider of all public services. Thus NPM calls for the rolling back of the State and rightsizing and downsizing of the government.

This new model has effectively supplanted the traditional model of public administration. The public sector in the future will inevitably be managerial both in theory and practice. It seems most unlikely that there will be a return to the traditional model of administration (Owen, p. 59)[30].

Defining Features/Characteristics of NPM

The OECD (Organization for Economic Cooperation and Development) countries have been trying to make their public sector more managerial through the introduction of "a more contractual, participative, discretionary style of relationship between levels of hierarchy; between control agencies and operating units; and between producing units, be they public or private. Instead of relying on rigid rules and hierarchical authority, most of these countries are following 'two broad avenues' to improve production and delivery of public goods and services (OECD, 1991, p. 11)[31].

The first avenue is: Raise the Production Performance of Public Organisations to improve the management of human resources including staff development, recruitment of qualified talent and pay-for-performance; involve staff more in decision-making and management; relax administrative controls while imposing strict performance targets; use information technology; improve feedback from clients and stress service quality; bring supply and demand decisions together (e.g. through charging users).

The second avenue is: "Make greater use of the private sector [to] promote a dependable, efficient, competitive and open public procurement system for contracting out production of publicly provided goods and services and contracting in intermediate goods and services; and, end monopoly or other protection for suppliers."

According to Christopher Hood (1991)[32] NPM comprises seven main features. They are:

1. Hands on professional management in the public sector. It means giving freedom/discretion to managers to manage. For 'accountability requires clear assignment of responsibility for action.'
2. Explicit standards and measures of performance. This requires goals to be defined and performance targets to be set because accountability requires a clear statement of goals and efficiency requires a 'hard look' at objectives.
3. Greater emphasis on output controls. Resources are directed to areas according to measured performance, because of the need to stress results rather than 'procedures'.
4. A shift to disaggregation of units in the public sector. This involves the breaking up of large entities into corporatised units around products, funded separately and dealing with one another on an 'arm's length' basis. This is justified by the need to create manageable units and to gain the efficiency advantage of franchise arrangements inside as well as outside the public sector.
5. A shift to greater competition in the public sector. This involves "the move to term contracts and public tendering procedures" and is justified as using "rivalry as the key to lower costs and better standards."
6. A stress on private sector styles of management practice. This involves a move away from military style 'public service ethic' and 'flexibility in hiring and rewards', and is justified by 'need to use 'proven' private sector management tools in the public sector.
7. A stress on greater discipline and parsimony in resource use. This involves "cutting costs, raising labour discipline, resisting union demands, limiting compliance costs to business and is typically justified by the need to check

resource demands of public sector and 'do more with less'.

In the words of Owen Hughes[33] there are four kinds of changes that constitute the managerial programme: Changes to focus on outputs; alterations to administrative inputs such as hiring staff by contracts; changes to the scope of government agencies; and changing accountability relationships with the political leadership and public, as managers become more responsible for results.

1. Changes to Focus on Outputs

The new catchphrase of governmental agencies should be the achievement of their objectives. This calls for a five-step strategy. First, the organization determines its overall strategy and sets objectives, with the participation of its various parts. Secondly, programmes are devised to attain the objectives specified by the strategy. A programme is a step by step process to achieve an objective. In the traditional model, programmes were not identified in a clear manner. Thirdly, the adoption of Planning-Programming Performance Budgeting System (PPBS) through which the structure of the organization, its staff and its budget will be determined. PPBS calls for activity based budget, funds, and personnel to carry out the work, whereas in the traditional model, based on the line-item budget, only inputs into the administrative process were spelled out and not the activities essential for achieving the outputs of the organization. Fourthly, performance at all levels needs to be measured to determine if the programme is being a carried out efficiently, effectively and economically to avoid time and cost overturns. In the traditional system even the performance measurement was at a low level and did not provide adequate information to policy-makers, nor did it facilitate rewarding those doing good work and warning or counselling those who were not doing their work well. Finally, there is need to evaluate the achievement of objectives without which precious resources will be simply wasted and projects will not be completed and results achieved.

2. Changes to Inputs

A number of changes in the inputs of the government agency (department) is called for in order to improve the incentives and thereby performance. According to Pollitt, (1990)[34] these changes include introduction of a regime of cash planning; staff cuts; adoption of a system of performance indicators emphasising economy and efficiency; individual staff appraisal on a more formal and extensive basis than had existed in the past; merit pay schemes linked to appraisal; financial devolution (budgetary responsibility) to line managers; emphasis on achievement of short-term targets and responsiveness to the consumer. The emphasis on performance is likely to lead to short-term appointments and termination of non-performing staff. These changes are advocated and buttressed by theoretical considerations from economics that organizations and individuals will not perform to their fullest capacity unless they are driven by incentives.

3. Reducing the Scope of Government

Cutting the scope of governments and bureaucracies is another aspect of the NPM. This will lead to reducing the number and range of functions and staff of the government—downsizing the bureaucracy through widespread privatization and contacting out of public service activities, introducing competition etc.

4. Relationships with Politicians and Public

Unlike in the traditional public administration model entailing separation between those giving orders (politicians) and those carrying them out (bureaucrats/civil servants), in the NPM model, since the responsibility for achievement of results is taken by the managers, the relationship between managers and politicians and managers and the public must alter. In the words of Bozeman and Straussman (1990)[35]:

Public management is not identical to government management or to public administration. Public management involves management under the influence of political authority...(positive or negative for the organization)...Political authority leaves its stamp on organizations in any of a variety of forms: red-tape (or, depending on your perspective, public accountability), shared power and independence, fragmentation, sensitivity to political cycles. The result is that public management is distinctive from management not similarly influenced by political authority.

As Rainey argues[36]:

In some cases and at some levels, public managers act with relative autonomy from political intervention, on the basis of technical rationality. In other times and places, political interventions are dominant. In still other instances, political and administrative criteria are effectively blended.

In other words, major skills are required of a public manager to play the role of a bureaucratic politician, to be able to interact with politicians and the public in a way, which is beneficial both to oneself and the organization. An effective manager is one who is a good political player. It must be remembered that "public service is a political institution and that public servants must operate in a political environment." To follow the political goals is the main function of any public service worthy of the name. The traditional model tried to depoliticise what is essentially political. NPM recognises the essential political character of government; public servants work with politicians in an interactive process called management. Undoubtedly, politicians have the final say, but the artificial separation of policy-making from administration has been discarded under NPM.

Likewise the public manager has a direct-responsibility to the public. He must be responsive, client-friendly and satisfy the demands of clients and outside groups.

In short, NPM is a 'marriage' of two different streams of ideas—one partner is 'the new institutional economies' (New Right)—the post-World War II development of public choice, transactions cost and principal-agent theories. It generated a set of administrative reform ideas such as public good vs. private good, external cost, decision-making cost, user choice, transparency and emphasis on incentive structures. They are very different from the traditional military-bureaucratic ideas of 'good administration' with their emphasis on orderly hierarchies and elimination of duplication or overlap (Ostrom 1974).

The other partner in the marriage is the 'business-type managerialism' in the public sector, in the tradition of the international scientific management movement/Neo-Taylorism (Pollitt 1990). It paved the way for administrative reform based on the concept of professional management expertise as portable, paramount over technical expertise, requiring high discretionary power to the manager to achieve results and central and indispensable to organisational performance through development of appropriate cultures (Peters and Waterman 1982)[37] and active measurement of organisational outputs.

Critique of New Public Management

The phenomenon of Development Administration coined and exported from the United States and defined as 'administration of development and development of administration'—both having an egg and chicken type of relationship (Riggs 1970)[38]. This characterised the administration in developing countries like India for four decades during the period 1950s to 1980s. It had all the defining features of public management. To illustrate, development administration is change and result oriented, goal-specific, management-oriented, planning, programming, performance budgeting based, project management-centered, peoples' participation-oriented requiring change of attitude, behaviour and professionalism on the part of development bureaucracy and decentralised structures to plan, implement and evaluate development plans, programmes and projects with active participation and involvement of the public and citizen groups at every phase in the decision-making process. The development administrators/Development bureaucracy were trained in the use of modern management techniques and project management tools such as Planning Programming (Performance) Budgeting System (PPBS), Cost-Benefit Analysis, Discount Cash Flow Analysis, Critical Path Method (CPM), Zero-Based Budgeting and Programme Evaluation Review Technique (PERT). Nonetheless, strangely enough neither the Western public administrationists nor their Third World counterparts ever realised this commonality and failed to describe/designate/christen Development Administration as Public Management. Now, New Public Management is said to embody most of these very features is being exported to the developing countries by the developed West as part of the package of globalisation, privatization and marketization to developing nations!

NPM is looked upon as nothing but a sheer fad and fashion since 1980 onwards; it is all hype and no substance; and it is like the Emperor's New clothes in the well-known Hans Anderson's story. New managerialism has changed very little and old problems and weaknesses remain underneath.

NPM has damaged the public service since it cannot deliver on its central claim (due to its inability) to lower costs per units of service. Despite its professional claim to promote cheaper and better quality public goods and services for all, it has, in practice, turned out to be a "self-serving movement designed to promote the career interests of an elite group of new managerialists."

Contrary to its claim to be "a garment for all seasons", NPM cannot be a universally applicable doctrine—its claim of universality is false, and therefore, it cannot be sustained. Further, it is very difficult to agree with, let alone acting on the public choice theory's key assumption of comprehensive view of rationality that "A rational man must be guided by the incentive system within which he operates.... [This] carrot and the stick guide scientists and politicians as well as donkeys' (Stigler 1975, p. 171)[39] because the average human being is 'a bundle of emotions' and does not always act rationally. He is not always selfish, self-centered, but he is also sympathetic, kind, good hearted to the poor, weak, young and the old and displays the nobler side of human nature too.

Criticism of Public Choice Theory of Bureaucracy

Public choice arguments about bureaucracy are hardly proven and have been challenged including from within their own framework (Dunleavy, 1991)[40]. The question about bureaucrats maximising budgets to achieve their personal ends suffers from a marked lack of evidence. Since there are central agencies or senior officers who gain personal benefits by restricting the money going to others, there can hardly be an overall conspiracy to increase the agency's budget (Dunleavy, 1986)[41]. Also, bureaucrats are hardly in a position to spend on themselves any extra funds they may get for their agency. As Wilson argues: "One wonders why Niskanen thinks bureaucrats are so desirous of maximising their budgets if they can enjoy so few of the fruits (Wilson, 1989, p. 118)[42]. Also the theory may be most applicable to the United States, where agencies build separate political relationships with Congress and where fiscal responsibility is hard to locate. In the Westminister model based countries, funding is more directly controlled by the executive and central agencies and there are particular bureaucrats whose career paths are advanced by their ability to cut the budgets of other agencies.

There is increasing recognition even among economists that their notion of 'rational economic man' is too often 'introduced furtively and left under-specified' (Dunleavy 1991)[43]. Even if there is only a need to apply these assumptions to the average or aggregate there are greater problems when the area of application of these assumptions is further away from the strict market behaviour as in the case of bureaucracy (Owen)[44]

According to Owen, in this kind of criticism, bureaucracy is seen as somewhat sinister, as an all-purpose societal villain, as a traditional betenoire or 'some kind of alien force' (Goodsell 1983, p. 149)[45]. This view exaggerates the power of bureaucracy and disregards its public purpose. The case against bureaucracy at some points is extrapolated into a case against all government or all non-market entities, in all circumstances instead of pointing to more realistic problems in this kind of organization, or pointing to the places where it might work or those where it would not", (Owen, pp. 55-56)[46].

On the credit side, the strength of the NPM approach lies in providing some intellectual coherence to cutting the public service, as well as restructuring its management in addition to challenging several traditional public administration precepts such as politics-administration dichotomy, life time employment, promotion by seniority, terms and conditions of public employment, traditional accountability and the theory of bureaucracy itself as based on poor theoretical backing and lacking in providing adequate incentive for good performance.

REFERENCES

1. Pressman, Jefferey L. and Aaron B. Wildavsky, 1973, Implementation: How Great Expectations in Washington D.C. Are Dashed on Oakland Or, Why It's Amazing that Federal Programmes Work At All, This Being A Saga of Economic Development Administration (Berkley: University of California Press).
2. Barry Bozeman, (ed.), 1993, *Public Management: The State of the Art* (San Francisco: Jossey-Bass).
3. Donald F. Kettl and H. Brinton Milward, (eds.), 1996, *The State of Public Management,* (Baltimore and London. The Johns Hopins University Press).
4. Graham, Cole Blease and Hays, Steven W., 1991, "Management Functions and Public Administration—POSDCORB Revisited"

in Steven J. Ott, Albert C. Hyde and Jay M. Shafritz (eds.) *Public Management: The Essential Readings*, Chicago: Lyceum Books/ Nelson-Hall.

5. Owen E. Hughes, 1994, *Public Management and Administration: An Introduction,* London: Macmillan Press.
6. Pollitt, Christopher, 1990, *Managerialism and the Public Services: The Anglo-American Experience*, Oxford: Basil Blackwell.
7. Rainey, Hal G., 1990, "Public Management: Recent Developments and Current Prospects" in Naomi B. Lynn and Aaron Wildavsky (eds.) *Public Administration: The State of the Discipline*, Chattam NJ: Chalham House Publishers.
8. Hood, Christopher, 1991, "A Public Management for All Seasons?" *Public Administrations*, 69(l), pp. 3-19.
9. Ostrom, Vincent, 1974, *The Intellectual Crisis in American Public Administration*, Revised Edition, Alabama: University of Alabama Press.
10. Niskanen, William A., 1971, *Bureaucracy and Representative Government*, Chicago: Aldine Atherton.
11. Buchanan, James A. and Tullock, Gordon, 1962, *The Calculus of Consent: The Logical Foundation of Constitutional Democracy,* Ann Arbor: University of Michigan.
12. *Ibid.*
13. Osborne, David and Gaebler, Ted, 1992, *Reinventing Government: How the Entrepreneurial Spirit is Transforming the Public Sector,* Reading M.A.: Addison-Wesley.
14. Allison, Graham, 1982, "Public and Private, Management, Are They Fundamentally Alike in All Unimportant Respects" in Frederick S. Lane, (ed.) *Current Issues in Public Administration*, New York: St. Martin Press.
15. Bowman, Cliff and Asch, David, 1987, *Strategic Management* (London: Macmillan).
16. OECD, 1990, *Survey of Public Management Developments: 1990*, Public Management Committee (PUMA) (Paris: OECD).
17. Porter, Michael, 1990, *The Comparative Advantage of Nations,* (London: Macmillan).
18. OECD, 1990a, Financing Public Expenditures through User Charges. Occasional Papers on Public Management (Paris: OECD).

19. Porter, *op. cit.*
20. OECD, 1990b, *Public Management Development: 1990,* Paris: OECD.
21. Pollitt, Christopher, 1990, *Managerialism and the Public Services: the Anglo-American Experience*, Oxford: Basil Blackwell.
22. Peters, B. Guy, 1989, *The Politics off Bureaucracy*, Third Edition (New York: Longman).
23. Robin, Jack and Bowman, James, (eds.), 1984, *Politics and Administration*, Woodrow Wilson and American Public Administration, New York: Marcel Dekker.
24. Merton, Robert K., 1968, *Social Theory and Social Structure*, Third Edition New York: Free Press.
25. Crozier, Michel, 1964, *The Bureaucratic Phenomenon*, Chicago: University of Chicago.
26. Hayek, F.A., 1944, *The Road to Serfdom,* Chicago: University of Chicago.
27. Friedman, Milton and Friedman, Rose, 1980, *Free to Choose* (Harmondsworth: Penguin).
28. Lan, Zhiyong and Rosenbloom, David H. (1992) 'Editorial', *Public Administration Review*, 52, 6, 1992.
29. Pollitt, *op. cit.*
30. Owen, *op. cit.*
31. OECD (1991) Public Management Developments; 1991 (PUMA: Paris, OECD).
32. Hood, *op. cit.,* pp. 4-5.
33. Owen, *op. cit.,* p. 69.
34. Pollitt, *op. cit.,* p. 83.
35. Bozeman, Barry and Straussman, Jaffrey D., 1990, *Public Management Strategies,* San Francisco: Jossey-Bass.
36. Rainey, Hall G. *op. cit.,* p. 173.
37. Peters, Thomas J. and Waterman, Robert H., 1982, *In Search of Excellence*, New York: Warner Books.
38. Riggs, Fred W., 1970, *Frontiers of Development Administration*, Durham: Duke University Press.
39. Stigler, George, 1975, *The Citizen and the State,* Chicago: University of Chicago Press.
40. Dunleavy, Patrick, 1991, *Democracy, Bureaucracy and Public Choice: Economic Explanations Political Science*, London: Harvester Wheat sheaf.

41. Dunleavy, Patrick, 1986, "Explaining the Privatization Boom: Public Choice vs. Radical Approaches", *Public Administration*, 64, 1986, pp. 13-34.
42. Wilson, James Q., 1989, Bureaucracy: What Government Agencies Do and Why they Do It, New York: Basic Books.
43. Dunleavy, (1991), *op. cit.*, p. 4.
44. Owen, *op. cit.*, p. 55.
45. Goodsell, Charles, 1990, Emerging Issues in Public Administration", in Naomi B. Lynn and Aaron Wildavsky (eds.) *Public Administration: The State of the Discipline*, Chatham NJ: Chatham House Publishers.
46. Owen, p. 56.

5

New Public Management: Public Administration in Turmoil

MOHIT BHATTACHARYA

I am beholden to the Department of Public Administration and Human Resource Management of this University for inviting me to deliver the Professor P.A. James Memorial Endowment Lecture. Late Prof. James shared with me a common interest: Study of local government, particularly urban local government. With the passage of the 74th Constitutional Amendment, this sub-field of public administration demand more vigorous intellectual attention. And that will be the best way to commemorate the memory or an eminent intellectual who devoted so much of his attention to this field. My lecture today is focused on a different theme: an analytical review of public administration as it has been evolving in recent years. There are anxieties as well as potentialities, as we watch the proceedings with considerable interest. Our field, nevertheless, seems to be in disarray.

Despite the tortuous and unending debate on its disciplinary character, public administration as a special field of study has continued to retain its dynamism since the Wilsonian exhortation for a science of administration in the last century. The sources of dynamism could partly be traced to actual changes in the real world of governance under the impact of sweeping social change. In part, the roots of dynamism can also be traced to an ongoing search for conceptual and methodological tools on the part of scholars in the discipline. Being both event-pushed and thought-propelled, the discipline has in recent years been causing considerable anxiety among scholars who continue to oscillate between doom and euphoria[1]. To some, public administration is dead; the public sector analysis needs a different discipline[2]. To others, the discipline is now full blown and autonomous. It has been claimed that the absence of a well-knit boundary and considerable porosity of a discipline is symptomatic of its growth and cross-fertilization. Public administration being deeply engrossed in the intricacies of governance in a fast-changing world has willy-nilly to draw on various allied disciplines, and so long as this process of dynamic interaction with the diverse knowledge world would be continuing, this should be construed as a positive sign of progressive development of the discipline.

Traditional Public Administration

To refresh our memory, for traditional public administration approach to the Public Sector, we look for sources in Willoughby *Principles of Public Administration* (1927), Gulick and Urwick, *Papers on the Science of Administration* (1937), Dwight Waldo, *The Administrative State* (1948), etc.

Theoretical/normative principles were inspired by the writings of Woodrow Wilson, J.S. Mill and Max Weber; and the other dominant influence came from the Scientific Management School of the early twentieth century, and later from mainstream organisation theory.

According to the traditional public administration approach the basic principles that would govern the structure of administration, involving the institutional arrangement, motivation of public employees and the status of public interest, would be as under:

1. The tasks of public institutions are to be in the hands

of the administrators. Politics and administration are two different kinds of activities and their functionaries are different. Administration starts after the initial push coming from politics.

2. Administration is based on written documents, thus making the office (the bureau) the heart of modern government.
3. The tasks are organised on a continuous, rule-governed basis.
4. The rules that regulate work may be technical or legal, and for this purpose, trained officials are necessary.
5. The tasks are divided into functionally distinct parts, each furnished with requisite authority and sanctions.
6. Office and tasks are arranged hierarchically; the rights of control and compliance being specified. All other things being equal, there is preference for centralization.
7. The resources of the organisation are quite distinct from those of the members as private individuals.
8. The office holder cannot appropriate his/her office for private aims.
9. In performing the assigned tasks, the public employees are to accept their vocational role to fulfil their obligations with a sense of duty.
10. The guiding philosophy in the management of public sector is that of *public interest.* This sets limits to the influenced of self-interest in politics and administration.

This is the well known Weberian/Scientific management model with emphasis on structure, work division, power-differentiation, centralization and public-private distinction. The whole design is machine-like, rigid and impersonal. As is well known, there are stock objections to this model which need not be repeated here. Broadly speaking, *there have been three kinds of reactions to this traditional model:*

(a) The principles of traditional public administration are primarily 'normative', sounding like "proverbs".

(b) These are lacking in descriptive accuracy. As organisations differ in complexity and character, one-shot enumeration of 'principles' is naïve and unrealistic.

(c) The principles fail to identify mechanisms that are conducive to public sector effectiveness and efficiency. They do not have the capacity to explain how the public sector actually works. In fact, the principles are not empirically oriented and are deficient in operational details. The modern state organisation is two complex to be pushed into a list of simple principles.

Post-Weber/Post-Wilson conception of Public Administration

The features other than those identified in the classical public administration model are currently being emphasized on the basis of empirical studies of government administration. The new approaches to public institutions underline the importance of public policy-making, implementation and management within the overarching framework of liberal democracy. It is being suggested that the complexities involved in public policy-making and implementation call for a rethinking about human motivation and efficiency and effectiveness in the public sector.

More pointedly, it is being argued that the classical model of public administration was unconscionably oriented toward rationality, specialization and division of work, rigid hierarchical structure and centralization. Successful management of the public sector and efficient production organizational outputs could not be correlated with the principles of classical public administration. As the critics argue, the Weberian claim of bureaucracy representing highest extent of rationality did not fit in with the real life situation in public administration. In reality, as the critics point out, rational behaviour is not a typical feature of modern organizational life. Organisational rationality as some form of collective expression of reasoned behaviour is rather fuzzy and does not conform to real life practice in the process of governance. Public policy decisions are often a matter of myriad influences, pulls and pressures, and there are multiple actors influencing decisions.

In this context, the behaviour of Simon's 'administrative man' striving to achieve 'bounded rationality' is very relevant[3]. Acknowledging information and data scarcity, time constraint, perceptual limitations, the administrator seeks to eliminate certain alternatives and imagined outcomes in order that a course of action could be adopted purely pragmatically. Most public policy decisions, as Braybrooke and Lindbolm observed[4], involved multiple interest-reconciling, and hence essentially synthesizing and accommodating in nature. Rationality-maximization is not what is intended in the actual process of administering. The 'muddling-through' can be attributed to the nature of public ends or goals in administration, which are not always well-defined and fine-tuned. Even irrationality as a component of decision, under such circumstances, may not be ruled out.

The other point relating to specialization and division of work has been attacked as impractical and injurious to organisational health and productivity.

Post-Weberian view of public organisations has basically been 'people'-oriented as distinguished from structure-oriented, as successive research findings have pointed out that people in organisation matter more than formal organisational structure The classical principles of public administration had held the orthodox view that organisational productivity demanded mechanization and routinization of administrative work. The alternative view, rebutting the classical stand point, has been that instead of sharp delineation of work division and narrow specialization, the structuring principles must aim at employee job satisfaction, and for this purpose organisational work-layout must provide opportunities for employees to work in multiple roles in much more flexible structures. There is considerable research evidence, since the early studies of the human relations school that clearly shows that organisational productivity does not automatically flow from a grand organisational design defining and functions to be discharged and coordinating the activities of each employee by narrow specialization and division of work.

The classical public administration model has emphasized hierarchy as a structural design concept. Hierarchy means that power distribution and centralization have been built into the architecture of traditional public administration.

Contrastingly, it has now been well accepted in organisational analysis that a decentralized strategy is superior to centralized structure. It promotes adaptability, flexibility and mobilization of local initiative. Decentralisation permits lower level operating units to interpret rules and regulations to suit local needs and to innovate in changed situations. Also participative decision-making becomes a reality in a bottom-up approach that utilizes the full potential of people at basic operating levels and creates conditions for free flow of information within the organisation.

Contemporary view about public organisation is thus not a perfectionist one, as, in reality, there is no such thing as a rigid and pure model of administration. What happens in actual administrative situations is policy evolution, adjustment and adaptation to shifting circumstances and environmental demands and pressures.

Against this background, the new approach to public administration, superseding the traditional model, can be distinguished with the help of following features:

1. Politics-administration dichotomy is unrealistic, irrelevant and unworkable, as the actors on either side frequently change positions and the two activities intermesh in the practical world of governance.
2. In public institutional life, there is not such thing as purely rational decision-making. It is 'bounded (limited) rationality' that characterizes actual public decision-making.
3. In a hierarchy-ridden organisation, it is the top that dominates and the bottom has simply to obey and

submit. Top-down policy implementation does not in actuality, work; there cannot be automatic accomplishment of objectives in the public sector or in any sector. Bottom-up communication is helpful in implementation, trusting that basic operating units have the capacity to reinterpret and innovate in dynamic situational changes. Drawing on rich social science research evidences, it is now well accepted that public administration is best looked after by self-steering groups rather than closely supervised groups. Hierarchy is essentially power-oriented rather than work-oriented and is positively threatening in its operations.

4. As practical administration shows, successful public administration is rarely rule-bound. What matters is goal achievement and effectiveness, allowing employees to play multiple roles.
5. Centralization leads to rigidity. Hierarchy results in implementation deficit. Free flow of communication is impeded by rigid hierarchy and centralization of power.
6. Public institutions operate efficiently when decentralized, allowing lower level initiative and adjustment.
7. In public administration tendencies towards irrationality are not rare, as many actors and forces impinge upon decisions and compete for accommodation.
8. Public employees do not have any special type of motivation. In real life, they have often been found to act to maximize self-interests like income, prestige and power, rather than public interest.

Thus the old idea of public administration being unique requiring a sheltered bureaucracy employed for life is now under challenge. The question have been raised why the bureaucratic form of organization should have the monopoly to provide public goods and services. It has been alleged that bureaucratic failures, that are numerous in reality, affect the society badly both immediately and from long-term perspective as well. There are various options available for the delivery of public goods and services, and society may benefit from the many suppliers syndrome. It is not necessary that government should always assume the role of a direct provider of goods and services; instead governments may operate indirectly, allowing non-govern-ment agencies to operate directly in a wide range of social activities.

Rigid, rule-bound, and hierarchic public administration does not suit the needs of a dynamic situation demanding speedy action. In this respect, many of the flexible organizational designs and practices pioneered by the private sector may be profitably introduced in public administration system with suitable modifications. The public-private distinction should not be fetishised as a matter of orthodoxy. In the larger interest of societal development, the two sectors should mix freely and collaborate whenever necessary and feasible. Even healthy competition between them should be welcome to improve quality of performance and accelerate the pace of work.

It has been argued that administration must be accessible, transparent and accountable. The citizen has every right to question how public fund is being spent and whether he is getting his money's worth. The civil servant has to be result-oriented, responsible and responsive. The bureaucracy has enjoyed security and anonymity at the cost of transparency. There must be more openness in administration and accountability for whatever is done or not done.

Changes in Advanced Countries

In the 1980s and early 1990s, for a variety of reasons remarkable changes took place in public sector management practices in most advanced countries:

(a) Structurally, the change was from rigid, hierarchical and bureaucratic form of public administration to a flexible, market-based form of public management.

(b) The change was not merely in form/style. There was remarkable change in the role of government in society, and (ii) similarly, there was a change in government-citizenship relationship. These objective conditions engendered opportunities for the emergence of almost a new paradigm in public sector analysis.

The 1990s saw the emergence of a new model of public sector management. This has been variously called: 'Managerialism' 'New Public Management, market-based public administration', 'Entrepreneurial Government' etc. the thrust is toward a determined effort to implement the 3Es: Efficiency, Economy and Effectiveness.

The new public management has following salient features:

1. Focus on management, not policy—on performance appraisal and efficiency.
2. Desegregation of public bureaucracies into agencies which deal with each other on a user-pay basis.
3. Use of quasi-markets and contracting out to foster competition.
4. Cost-cutting.
5. A style of management which emphasizes, inter-alia, output targets limited term contracts, monetary incentives freedom to manage.

A more positive perspective, within this stream of thought is that of Osborne and Gaebler (*Reinventing Government*, 1992), who suggest a ten-point programme for what they call entrepreneurial government (EGs):

1. EGs promote competition between diverse providers of goods and service.
2. They *empower* citizens by pushing control out of bureaucracy.

3. They measure performance of heir agencies focusing particularly on outcomes, not inputs.
4. They are driven by their missions—not by their rules/regulations.
5. They redefine their clients as customers and offer them choices.
6. They prevent problems rather than cure them after they blow out.
7. They put their energy into earning money, not simply spending it.
8. They decentralize authority, embracing participatory management.
9. They prefer market mechanisms to bureaucratic mechanisms.
10. They focus not simply on providing public service, but on catalyzing all sectors—public, private, voluntary—into action to solve community problems.

These are fairly clear-cut straight identification marks of a type of government which the new inventors call 'entrepreneurial'. Although, the characteristic features are being bandied about as 'empirically derived', these are, more accurately, preferred qualities than actual attributes.

Reinventing Government immediately caught the attention of anti-bureaucracy campaigners, and the publication was accorded a warm welcome, heralding, as it were, the birth of a new form of public management.

Government Response: with considerable caution, the practical world of governance responded to this new paradigm change in the following manner:

- Improving public management through performance measurement and evaluation.
- Reducing Budgets.
- Cutting the size of government.
- Privatization of public enterprise.
- Contracting out in selective areas.

The overall emphasis has been on changing bureaucracies into result-oriented organizations, in which managers would be accountable for achieving targets and results. Reduction in the size of government reducing the functional load of bureaucracies, speed, results production and accountability soon become the buzz words. Historically, bureaucracy has always been under attack as power grabbers, secretive rule-bound and inward looking rather than client-oriented. But, the contemporary scenario seems unique in that it marks a savage onslaught on bureaucracy as the mains prong of mal-governance, as if other causes are of no consequence. The complexities of a post-modern society, the crumbling ideologies of politics and the overall social development puzzle of the dying century are, side pushed, and 'bureaucracy' is singled out as the villain of the piece.

As Caiden has summed up the situation: All blamed the dead hand of bureaucracy, especially the poor performance of public bureaucracies and the daily annoyances of irksome restrictions, cumbrous red-tape, unpleasant officials, poor service and corrupt practices.

The CAPAM Conference

In this context the inaugural conference of the Commonwealth Association for Public Administration and Management held in Charlottetown, Canada in August, 1994 assumes considerable significance. For the first time in the history of the Commonwealth such a high-level conference addressed itself exclusively to the issues of public management in today's context dubbed as 'government in transition'. There was a general consensus that strong environmental forces have been buffeting the public sector, and governments all over the world are being forced to cope with them. Some of the impinging forces are knowledge-based production, the communication revolution and a massive explosion in world trade. In a multi-polar world, trade negotiations need to be worked out both bilaterally and multilaterally. The information technology revolution has led to shrinkage of distances among partners and facilitated almost instant electronic networking. Globalisation has become a reality, setting the stage for professional networking and collaboration in the development and sustenance of a new public administration.

The 'new paradigm' that has emerged "emphasizes the role of public managers in providing high-quality services that citizens value, advocates increasing managerial autonomy, particularly by reducing central agency controls; demands measures, and rewards both organisational and individual performance; recognizes the importance of providing the human and technological resources that managers need to meet their performance targets, and is receptive to competition and open-minded about which public purposes should be performed by public servants as opposed to private sector".

The new paradigm has several interrelated components that cut across traditional ways of organising government. *The first component* relates to the delivery of high-quality services that citizens value. The consumers are reconceptualised as active customers and not just passive recipients. Hence, serious attempts are being made to find out what the customers expect. Public sector organisations, as in UK, Singapore and some other nations are setting performance targets, measuring performance and publicizing results for the wider public. The most dramatic such initiative is UK's citizens' charter, a global statement of the government's service quality commitments. This was launched by Prime Minister John Major in 1991. Singapore has set up a Service Improvement Unit (SIU) in the Prime Minister's office to keep a watch on departmental efforts.

The *second component* of the new paradigm emphasizes that to achieve high-quality standard of services, the managers need increased autonomy. In UK, Australia, New Zealand and Singapore, a distinct trend is noticeable toward shifting operating responsibilities from the central departments to specific agencies.

Infrastructural development is Singapore, for example, has been transferred to agencies with clear performance targets and increased autonomy. Also, greater flexibility in working conditions such as contractual appointments, work place bargaining etc. is being permitted to make use of more expertise and employee creativity.

Organisational structures are being simplified and hierarchies flattened to create conditions for more positive and productive managerial leadership. In the field of financial management, freedom to manage consolidated running costs of programmes is being accorded to managers in countries like UK and Australia. The general trend is to increase the autonomy of local managers by devolving more power to them.

The *third component* of the new paradigm relates to fairly rigorous performance measurement of individuals and organisations. Rewards including pay structures are based on fulfilment of performance targets. Both UK and New Zealand are moving from a tenure system to fixed-term contracts. In financial management, agencies are changing from cash to accrual accounting, thus making them more cost-conscious and resource-saving. In Canada, Australia and UK, periodic review of government programmes has become almost customary.

The *fourth component* concerns managerial support services to facilitate achievement of pre-set performance targets. Successful managerial performance needs to be backed up by proper human and technological resources. In the area of human resource management, recruitment policy has to be directed toward drawing the best available talent from the market, assuring them attractive salary and other allied benefits, and constantly exposing them to skill-improving training programmes. Australia is using competency-based training that starts by defining competencies relevant to a given organisational level. UK and Mauritius are tailoring training to rank.

Equity initiatives are being taken up in some countries. For instance, Australia has drawn up a strategic plan targeted at women, the disabled, the aboriginal and those with non-

English backgrounds. This is expected to expand the pool of talent available to the government.

It is being increasingly recognised that leading edge information technology is an essential facilitator of service improvement initiatives. By 1990, Singapore civil service described itself as being fully computerized. Both for internal communication and service provision, information technology is spreading fast in many commonwealth countries.

Alongside the need for autonomy for agency/departmental management, it is also being asserted that managerial performance at any level has to be responsive to the overall, central policy directives. The organisation of the Cabinet has thus been streamlined in many countries. Australia has established systems of Cabinet Committees, reduced the number of departments, and grouped programmes more rationally. Some of the commonwealth countries have recognised institutions for giving support to Cabinet functioning. Jamaica has created a Permanent Secretaries Board and facilitated Cabinet review of key areas of administration.

The *fifth component* of the new paradigm is an advocacy of "receptiveness to competition and an open-mined attitude about which purposes should be performed by the public sector as opposed to the private sector". In many commonwealth countries, there is currently more and more private sector involvement in activities that were formally reserved for the public sector. In the field of infrastructure development such as roads, electricity etc., private sector is being invited to undertake constructional and extension activities. Non-government organisations are taking up projects in many countries (e.g. India) in the social sector (specially health, education, nutrition and child health and women's development). In Bangladesh, the role of the Grameen Bank in providing micro-credit to the rural poor, particularly women, has attracted international attention.

'Privatization' has been adopted as an official policy in some of the nations. In Singapore telecom, airlines and shipyards have been privatized. UK has gone ahead with an aggressive policy of privatization (47 privatizations since 1979). There are also examples of public-private joint ventures in some countries (e.g. Singapore, India), removing in the process the traditional rigidity about the 'public' sphere.

Policies supportive of private sector activities have been adopted in most commonwealth countries. Important among these are dismantling price controls, deregulation and narrowing down of the public sector (also called downsizing).

An Overview

The new paradigm of public management with its explicit 'market'-orientation and over reliance on the private sector has varied responses form the Commonwealth countries. It looks as though neo-classical economics has captured the public sector all over the world.

The negative feelings toward government and the public sector so dominant in the eighties, have, however, now been changing; and there is growing concern today about government's crucial role in macro-management and in creating sound policy environment for the society and the economy to function smoothly. Government has to lead the whole socio-economic system and find alternative ways of providing services and facilities. It is good to know how private management works; but at the same time the unique policy role of the higher civil service should not be diluted in our craze for phone managera-lism. Government, especially at the higher echelons, has its peculiar ways of accommodating interests, feeling the pulse of the nation, intervening in conflictual situations and calculating pay-offs in difficult bargaining situations.

Above all, there is a thing called 'public interest' which lies at the heart of government operations, and it is irreplaceable by an market philosophy.

The other point of view that has come up sharply in the CAPAM conference is the need for strengthening the civil society in many of the developing countries. Operating almost as a third sector there are institutions run and sustained by citizens, sometimes with assistance and advice from NGOs. Countries in the developing world have to build infrastructural facilities, improve people's access to resources, and conserve natural resources by promoting sustainable use 'Empowering' citizens assumes crucial significance in this context. Outside the sphere of big government and macro-management, there are the grass roots people's efforts to organise themselves against deprivation and exploitation from above. The new paradigm of public management is centred on the core and almost oblivious of the periphery. There is, therefore, a lurking suspicion that the new paradigm might as well lead to hijacking of the state by the 'private' and the 'powerful'. The 'public' sphere may ultimately remain only with the grass roots where people strive hard in their own way to build a democratic space away from the big state's massive management enterprise.

The CAPAM conference came out with a new paradigm of public management no doubt. But, there were voices also, suggesting alternative ways of organising government. Narrowing down the scope of government, it was pointed out, may not be the universal recipe, in view of the diverse development trajectories of nations.

The new public management philosophy was basically triggered by a combination of economic issues and geo-political changes (collapse of the second world) resulting in reduced financial resources for governments. Managerial rethink, therefore, became an imperative necessity to optimize scarce resource use and find alternative ways of delivering public services by developing a new synergy between the public and private sectors. As Mohan Kaul has summed up: "the broad objectives of these reforms have been to shift emphasis from developing plans to developing key strategic areas, to shift emphasis from inward-looking systems to developing partnerships, to shift emphasis from inputs and processes to outputs and outcomes; and to shift emphasis towards managing diversity within a unified public service. Finally, managerial pragmatism and political conviction are highlighted as essential to motivating management innovation in government."

Relevance for India

Does the new paradigm in any way influence Indian administration? For an answer to this question, one has to look back to the massive output of the last Administrative Reforms Commission. The voluminous reports of the Commission, as is well known, were put in cold storage. It was expected that coming in the wake of 'structural adjustment' and globalisation-liberalisation policy of the government, the Fifth Pay Commission would be ushering in an era of 'new public management'. Note the Commission's visionary zeal.

Public services have to subserve the new goals of the state. From mere controllers and regulators, they have to get converted into catalysts, promoters and facilitators. Their numbers to be right sized and an officer-orientation brought about. Government itself needs to be restructured by closing down departments or amalgamating them, by transferring subjects and institutions to the State Governments and Panchayati Raj bodies, by converting departmental undertakings into public sector undertakings, by encouraging cooperatives, autonomous bodies and non-governmental organisations to take over some of the functions of the State. Simultaneously, the Government office needs to be reinvented.

"Reinventing Government" seems an infectious phrase! In terms of implementation, however, the government has again come a cropper. Reportedly, the Ninth Plan size has to be cut to make room for the sustenance of the Leviathan! Public management in India represents a classic case of bureaucratic-political self-aggrandizement at the expense of public interest. Meanwhile, India's future remains mortgaged to the past!

REFERENCES

1. *Government in Transition*, The Inaugural Conference of the Commonwealth Association for Public Administration and Management, Charlotttown, Prince Edward Island, Canada, 28-31 August, 1994, University of Toronto Press, 1995.
2. Mohan Kaul, "The New Public Administration: Management Innovation in Government", *Public Administration and Development,* Vol. 17, 13-26, 1997.
3. Ewan Ferlie, Andrew Pettigrew, Lynn Ashburner, Louise Fitzerald, *The New Public Management in Action,* OUP, 1996.
4. Jan-Erik Lane, *The Public Sector: Concepts, Models and Approaches,* SAGE, 1993.

6

Implementation of New Public Managament: Problems and Prospects

R.K. SAPRU AND P.M. BORA

New Public Management is the new reform being widely accepted by all kinds of administrative systems all over the world. It is a 'new' combination of 'public' and 'management'—a combination of concepts taken both from 'public administration' and 'business management'. New public management aims at adoption of management technique developed and successfully tested in the private sector for the efficient, economical and effective functioning of public administration as an instrument of 'collective problem solving'. New Public Management is the utilitarian merger of the normative orientation of public administration and the instrumental orientation of private management. It takes 'what' and 'why' from politico-administrative system and 'how' from the business world. It marks a beginning of an aggressive wholesale induction of core value of business management into public administration.

New Public Management' called as 'Managerialism', 'Market-based Public Administration', 'entrepreneurial government' is the process of 're-inventing government' which emerged in the beginning of the last decade in response to the challenges of globalization, international competitiveness and technological changes. New Public Management represents a paradigm shift from 'traditional' model to a 'managerial' model of public administration, which is accessible, accountable, transparence responsive and flexible; which aims at reducing the bureaucracy, giving priority to the consumers and empowering the employees: which saves government money increases efficiency of government managers and reduces the 'red tape'. Osborne and Gaebler call this as 'entrepreneurial government' or a 'governmental market'.[1]

Gone are the days when the machinery of public administration was considered to be the only one sure solution of all our problems. In the beginning of 1970s, the entire developing world started feeling disillusioned with the functioning of the public bureaucracies. This caused serious introspection among the think tanks as well as the policy makers. It was realized that the traditional administration is based on normative 'proverb like' principles, which lack in accuracy as well as mechanism for ensuring effectiveness and efficiency. It was also felt that the Wilsonian politics-administration dichotomy is absolutely unrealistic unworkable and irrelevant; that purely rational decision are impossible in real working situations; that rigid and hierarchy-based top-down pyramid of administration is both non-existent and non-workable; that rule-bound centralized bureaucracies systems have failed to deliver satisfactory public services; that the civil services are neither motivated to serve public interest nor ready to adjust with changing time; that instead of being an effective instrument of public welfare and socio-economic upliftment of the people, the public bureaucracies have become self-centered, self-seeking and selfish instrument of autocratic, an-accountable, even expanding burgeoning bureaucracy seeking promotions, power, money and prestige and that the monopoly of public administration has to be challenged to end its tyranny. Hence it became absolutely necessary to totally transform the existing traditional public administration. The call to reverse the trend and reform the administration came from President Ronald

Regain in U.S.A. and Prime Minister Margaret Thatcher in U.K. New Public Management (NPM) is the latest concept to enter the lexicon of Public Administration aiming to transform it completely. It has been now accepted all over the world that "...we do not need more government we need better governance...collectively solving our problems. Government is the instrument...it is out-dated...it is time to remake it."

The emergence of the new managerial approach in the public sector marks a shift from earlier reforms. Instead of reforming the public administration. New Public Management represents the total transformation of the entire public sector and its relationship with government, bureaucracy and society. When it was found that the traditional public administration did not work any more, then the governments began to hire trained managers, borrowed management techniques from the private sector, erased the line between public and private sectors, set to change working environment, put their energy into maximum cost reduction as well as earning some profits and catalyzed all sectors—public, private and voluntary—into action to provide best public services of the choice of the customers. In short we can say that by doing this the government try to make their public sectors more managerial in nature—Osborne and Gaebler set out a ten-point programme for what they term as 'entrepreneurial government (NMP).

Most entrepreneurial government promote competition between service providers. They empower citizens by publishing control out of the bureaucracy into the community. They measure the performance of their agencies, focusing not on inputs but on outcomes. They are driven by their clients as customers and offer them choices. They prevent problems before they emerge, rather than simply offering services afterwards. They put their energy into earning money not simple spending it. They decentralize authority embracing participatory management. They prefer market mechanisms to bureaucratic mechanisms. And they focus not simply on providing public services but on catalyzing all sectors—public, private and voluntary—into action to solve their community's problems. New Public Management simply stands for all the above elements.

Theoretical Basis

Unlike traditional public administration founded on (i) the theory of bureaucracy, and (ii) the theory of separation between politics and administrations. New Public Management (NPM) is theoretically based on economics and private management. Pollit, for example, argues that management is "clearly an activity which is intimately concerned with directing flows of resources so as to achieve defined objectives" and these objectives "are defined predominantly in the language of economic." At another point he claims the driving force behind management change was a generic model of management' and the particular species of generics tended to be 'of a new-Taylorian character.'[2]

It is argued that the economic basis to managerialism allows it to draw on 'public choice theory' (1980s). The key assumption of public choice is the view of individual rationality. According to Stigler: "A rational man must be guided by the incentive system within which he operates.... The carrot and the stick guide scientists and politicians as well as donkeys."[3]

The 'public choice theory' gave theoretical backing to the attack on bureaucracy, politicians (motivated by selfish instead of public interest) reducing government in general and gave a methodology for designing market oriented public policies. Economic thinking dominated the government and public administration in both theory and practice. The focus on managerial models on results, productivity and measurement could be said to derive from economics and private management.

It may be emphasized that public management has largely been influenced by the theories and techniques of private management. Much more attention now paid to the strategic planning and management in the public sector is attributed to the private sector. What is observed more often is the adoption of private sector personnel practices including the greater use of rewards throughout the organization, such as paying more for good performance, or less for poor performance, or terminating staff relatively easily (the voluntary retirement schemes have been offered to the staff working in the public sector banks and many public enterprises in India recently), new public management looks at results first, with no preconceived notion as to how these occur.

Thus economics and private management do largely contribute to the formation of theoretical bases of New Public Management. Two issues which have direct relevance to the NPM practice are: (i) Relationship with politicians, and (ii) New contractualism.

(i) *Relationships with Politicians*: In traditional model of public administration, the relationship between the political leadership and the bureaucracy was one of the master and servant, or one giving the order and one carrying it out. The main characteristics of the NPM approach is that responsibility is taken by managers for the achievement of result. Public managers are now involved in matters of policy; they are equally involved in matters of strict politics, and they are more often personally accountable if something goes wrong. An effective manager is one who is a good political player. The traditional model attempted to de-politicize what is essentially political. New Public Management, on the other hand, does recognize the essential political character of government managers and the public servants are supposed to work with politicians in an interactive process. Further, there is the recognition of the need for direct relationship between public managers and the public.

(ii) *New Contractualism*: Any government service can be provided by contract either externally through private providers or internally with other parts of government, "Contracting can replace traditional bureaucratic hierarchy and command with networks of providers loosely clustered around government funding agencies delivering services once the exclusive domain of the State."[4] The resort to contracts is to reduce the scope of the public sector. Devis adds that a contract state might turn being a kin to the traditional model of public administration, containing small elite of core officials.

Driving Paradigms

New Public Management has driving paradigms-(l) providing responsive services efficiently, (2) developing competition and choice, (3) ensuring performance control, accountability and transparency, (4) devolving authority and providing flexibility, (5) improving the management of human and other resources, (6) optimizing information technology, (7) improving the quality of regulation and cost-effectiveness of the products, (8) strengthening the 'steering' functions rather than 'rowing'.

In the present context when the society that is emerging finds itself embroiled, in global competition. Information Technology is revolutionizing the society instantaneous communication is the order of the day, the society is becoming more and more knowledge based, the weberian bureaucracies with their universal attitudes of mediocrity, inflexibility, obsession with authority are utterly incapable inadequate and unsuitable to respond to the demands and challenges if such an age, the only alternative model to replace the government is the 'entrepreneurial government' which is based on the paradigms and principles of New Public Management (NPM). David Osborne and Ted Gaebler prescribe the following ten principles of entrepreneurial governance:

1. Government should form out as many activities to the

private sector as possible. It should find out alternatives to in-house delivery such as contracting out, entering into public-private partnerships and utilizing such devices as vouchers, volunteers, seed money etc.

2. Competition among government agencies must be encouraged. Competition should be injected into the governing process by encouraging bidding for tasks, internal rivalry among sub-units and competition among services for clients.
3. Public agencies should minimize the number of rules by which they operate. Items to be eliminated are the line item budget, year-end fund expiration ('rule and lapse' in financial administration'), and too elaborate job classification.
4. Professional administrators should not be given exclusive responsibility for running all aspects of programmers. Participative system of management should be observed. Clients should be empowered by encouraging their participation in governing councils and management teams.
5. Agency performance should be reviewed not on the basis of inputs but on the basis of output. Policy-outcomes should be the yardstick of performance measurement.
6. Clients should be viewed as customers. They should be given choices. Public agencies should be client-friendly. Employees must be suitable trained in customer contact. There should be introduced test marketing and suggestion forms.
7. Government's image of being a mere spending mechanism must change. It should not just spend money, but earn it as well. It should invoke the devices of user fees, shared savings, enterprise funds, entrepreneurial loan pools, internally competitive profit centers.

8. On the analogy of 'prevention is better than cure', public agencies should not just deliver services to meet needs, but prevent needs from arising. Examples are fire prevention, anti-smoking campaign, preventive maintenance etc.
9. Centralized agencies and institution should become decentralized. The traditional hierarchical structure should be abandoned, viding way to developing authority, teamwork, participatory management, labour management cooperation, quality circles and employee development programmes.
10. Government should not attempt to achieve its ends only by command and control, but also by restructuring market. Examples could be subsidized health insurance, incentives for dispersal of industries from city area etc.

All the features of New Public Management or Entrepreneurial Government so far mentioned above, provide a fairly clear-cut and straight forward identification marks of a new multi-faceted governance system. Prof. Mohil Bhattacharya identified it as (1) catalytic government, (2) community-owned government, (3) competitive government, (4) mission-driven government, (5) result oriented government, (6) customer-driven government, (7) decentralized government and (8) market-oriented government.[5]

Since the 1990s, many of the above aspects of New Public Management, managerialism or market-based public administration are being followed by most developed as well as developing countries. India is no exception. In order to deliver high quality service that citizens value public organizations are setting high performance targets, measuring performances, publicizing the result, taking initiatives to formulate Citizen's Charters and Service Improvement Units. In order to make more flexibility and autonomy available to the public managers operational responsibilities are being shifted to suitable agencies and measures like the contractual staff hiring, work place bargaining to make use of their expertise and creativity, structural simplification flattening the hierarchies, cost-cutting exercises and devolution of more powers to local level managers are being adopted. Fair and rigorous performance appraisals of both the individuals and organizations, performance related rewards and pay structures, fix-term contract systems, more cost-conscious and customary. Improved human resource management practices, provision of excellent technological resources, computerization moves, constant skill improving competency based training and expansion of talent search operations are some of the initiatives being taken in many countries. In many countries there is more and more private sector involvement in many activities like the infrastructure development, like roads, electricity etc. and social sector like the health, nutrition, child and woman development, education etc. In many countries 'privatization' of many public sectors like telecom, airlines, shipping, oil exploration, etc. has become an official policy. Public-private joint ventures are also being established. Along with dismantling of controls, deregulation of public sector, downsizing of public bureaucracies and de-bureaucratization of public administration is rapidly becoming the order of the day. What has emerged is a more flexible and open-ended vision of Governance in this age of globalization, liberalization and privatization.

Implementing New Public Management

In developing countries like India, where capital markets are not fully developed and where even now, the public bureaucracy remain more important than in western countries, implementation of New Public Management has to face many challenges and problems. There is likely to be greater domination of foreign or multinational corporations or changing from public bureaucracy to market-based management may lead to increase in the corrupt practices. For the market-based changes to work the public bureaucracy will resist to give up its substantial power—that too voluntarily. Lack of experience in the operation of markets, which requires complete observance of rule of law, rule of competition and sterile compliance of contracts poses serious problems in developing countries where goal are vague and unclear or where corruption is endemic. Contracting out is not likely to be successful in such countries because many ethical problems may arise relating to contracting our practices as well as public officials giving contracts. Political interference can not be ruled out. In fact there are greater opportunities for the unethical, the dishonest and the corrupt with the acceptance of new managerialism.

Most developing countries are faced with problems of poverty, illiteracy, unemployment, inequalities, gender-bias, rule of law, inadequacy of capital imperfect market, lack of suitable human resources and heterogeneous socio-cultural environment. In such situations the assumptions that the government is a market that the 'citizen' is a 'customer', that 'downsizing' will decrease the 'cost' of governance without diminishing its effectiveness, and that the public bureaucracy is the primary cause of several ills, do not sound to be correct. There is a possibility that by reinventing government, the governance in countries like India, "could possible become more complicated, less effective, more authoritative and ultimately weaker and unsuccessful in serving its citizens."[6]

In countries like India, the government's crucial role in providing social services, in leading the entire socio-economic systems, in creating sound policy environment for its smooth functioning and in macro-management can not be overlooked. Government accommodate varying interests, feel the pulse of the nation, intervene in conflictual situations, conserve natural resources, promote sustainable access to resources, work against deprivation and exploitation and make 'justice' possible. No market philosophy, no new paradigm of public management can hijack these core 'public duties' of the state. They lie at the heart of government operations and are irreplaceable by any market/management philosophy.

In the soul-searching contemporary Public Administration the waves of reforms are sweeping through the public sector under the societal pressures, international demands and national interests. Let us welcome all these new waves without forgetting that public bureaucracy, managerialism and democratic polity are needed in a liberal democratic society. As long as democracy is valued, the big questions of Public Administration must go beyond the big questions of Public Management.

REFERENCES

1. Osborne and Gaebler, *Reinventing Government*, Addison Wesley, 1992, p. 20.
2. Charstopener Pollit, *Management and Public Services, The Anglo American Experiences,* OXFORD, 1990, p. 5.
3. George Stigler, *The Citizen and the State*, Chicago University of Chicago Press. 1975, p. 171.
4. Giya Davis 'Implications, Consequences and Futures', in Davis *et al.*, (eds.), *The New Contractralism* (Mel borne Macmillan 1977), p. 236.
5. Mohil Bhattacharya, *New Horizon of Public Administration*, Jawahar Publication and Distributors. New Delhi 2000, pp. 375-376.
6. R.K. Sapru, *Development Administration* (2nd edition). Sterling Publishers, New Delhi, 2003. p. 386.

7

Understanding New Public Management in Contemporary Times

R.N. PRASAD

The conventional public administration is theoretically rooted in Wilsonian dichotomy of politics and administration, Weberian theory of bureaucracy and the other dominant influence coming from the scientific management school of the early 20th century (Taylorian) norms of work and later from mainstream organization theory has been in turmoil. The outcomes of traditional public administration include bloated but inefficient, self-centred, self seeking and selfish bureaucracy, nexus between the tri-politicians, bureaucrats and pressure groups for covetous interests, alienation of public from administration and increasing financial burden of administrative machinery on the state exchequer. Not only but they existing bureaucracy is always after promotions, power, prestige and money. Hence the monopoly of unaccountable public administration needs to be challenged to end its autocracy/tyranny. So to reform the conventional public administration became an imperative need. The alternative model of the centralized governance is the New Public Management which emphasizes less and better governance, downsizing and reorganization of government. These initiatives based on the philosophy of NPM have been taken in the advanced, newly industrialized as well as developing countries. Briefly New Public Management being a new reform strategy has been accepted in all types of administrative systems all over the world. It is a new combination of public and management—a combination of concepts taken both from public administration and business management. New Public Management has adopted management techniques which have been developed and successfully tested in the private sector for the efficient, economical and effective functioning of public administration as an instrument of collective problem solving. Thus, New Public Management is called as managerialism, market based public administration, entrepreneurial government owing to the process of reinventing government that has emerged in the beginning of last decade in response to the challenges of globalization, international competitiveness and technological changes. The New Public Management is theoretically based on economics and private management.

As regards, the theoretical foundations of the NPM many developed and newly industrialized countries have brought about a lot of administrative innovations as an integral part in their administrative systems which, Hood has codified these administrative reforms/innovations as the New Public Management which has the following salient features such as free to manage in the public sector, standards and measures of performance, emphasis on output than procedures, shift to disaggregation of units in public sector, greater competition in public sector, emphasis on private sector styles of management practice and stress on greater discipline and parsimony in resource use. Besides, this administrative reforms lay stress on managerialism, market based public administrative, post-bureaucratic paradigm and entrepreneurial government.

David Osborne and Ted Gaeblor in his book Reinventing Government have suggested ten principles for re-inventing government as under:

Catalytic Government, steering rather than rowing community owned government: empowering rather than serving competitive government: injecting competition into service delivery mission driven government transforming rule driven organization, result oriented government: funding outcomes, not inputs, consumer driven government, meeting the needs of the customers not the bureaucracy, enterprising government earning rather than spending, anticipatory government: preventive rather than cure, decentralized government from hierarchy to participation and team work and market oriented government—leveraging change thought the market.

Some notable schools like New Right School of Thought, Public Choice School led by Black, Buchanan, Tullock and Niskanen, Chicago, School led by Fried man, Austrian School led by Hayek and supply side Economics School led by Laffer, Gilder, Wanniski and Business type managerialism and management literature have supported the principles of the NPM. For instance, to New Right School of Throught the involvement of the state leads to increasing monopoly, increasing budget and suppressing of entrepreneurial behaviour, limiting choice.

As regards the suggestions of the New Right School, the role of the state as a regulator and producer needs to be reduced. Deregulation and privatization as reforms are suggested. Other measures include the reduction of inflation, lower taxation, increasing role of market forces in the provision of public services and institutional and constitutional reforms. These reforms promote competition between rival bureaucracies, reduce the influence of interest groups and corporate institutions and impose a constitutional upper limit on public expenditure as a proportion of the gross national product.

Keeping in view the nature and aim of the NPM in practice, various administrative reforms such as reorganization and downsizing of the Government, creation of senior civil services, adoption of private sector styles of management practice, promotion of customer oriented administration. Structurally the change is from rigid hierarchical and bureaucratic form of public administration to a flexible market based form of public administration. The thrust of NPM is to implement three things—efficiency, economy and effectiveness. It focuses on management, performance appraisal, efficiency, evaluation and not policy, cost cutting, reducing budget and contracting out in selective areas.

The new public management philosophy has been triggered by a combination of economic issue and geo-political changes (collapse of the second world) resulting in reduced financial resources for government. Hence managerial rethink becomes an imperative need to increase scarce resource use and find alternative ways of delivering public services by developing a new synergy between public and private sector. Briefly, shift from inputs and procedures to outputs and outcomes is laid stress/emphasis on managerial pragmatism and political conviction are highlighted as essential to motivating management innovation in government.

As regards the implementation of the market based public administration approach, market based reform and re-inventing government in India, it seems infeasible due to the bureaucratic-politician self-aggrandizement at the expense of public interest. Besides, the change involves a paradigm shift from the role of government, relationship between politicians and administrators, abilities and qualities needed for public servants, method of their selection and accountability factor. As a result, there will arise three problems: political, legal and constitutional. It may not be possible to implement in all areas. The areas need to be defined/identified keeping in view the nature of the Indian society, predominant rural character/nature of the Indian society, the socio-economic interest of the vast Indian masses living below poverty line. Moreover, the markets are not natural friends of people, they have to be made people friendly through government interventions.

Further there are basic problems of agriculture, health and education to be tackled. So there is a time to wait and see to what extent administered reforms can be adopted so that new organization and structure may be involved to tackle these problems and whether business houses will invest in these areas substantially.

8

New Public Administration vs. New Public Management

S.P. VERMA

India and China the modem worlds giants not only have come to be regarded as the two nations going to dominate the world scene in the 21st century. These two also represent two ancient cultures going back to thousands of years. To most of us, Public Administration as understood in modem times represents systems, methods and practices initiated by Anglo-Saxons. However, as long back as 500 BC Confucius teachings had not laid down the basic ideas for administrators reflecting guidelines as to how the Chinese administrators must think, feel and act but also laid down principles and methods to select the Mandarins (Civil Servants).

Similarly, Kautilya in his Arth sastra about 300 BC had already written about training of state officials. "Both Indian and Chinese pioneers stressed values of service and accountability which need emphasis up to this day. With the official rejection of the teachings of Confucius in his home land and the systematic omission of pre-colonial heritage in the rest of Asia the influences of these and other attempts to educate public officials on contemporary theory and practice of Public Administration remain largely unacknowledged." (Carino).

More formal efforts towards educating civil servants in Asia began in the 19th and early 20th centuries. For example the college of Fort William at Calcutta (1800), subsequently to become a model for Hailey Bury College in UK (1806).

It was the article "The Study of Administration" by Woodrow Wilson published in Political Science Quarterly 2, 3 (June 1887) which many regard as the beginning of Modern Public Administration. It has been a long march, almost a century and two decades (1887 till 2005), for the discipline of Public Administration to traverse through various phases. In between the World was witness to two World Wars the birth and decay of Communist World, the Korean War (1951), the end of Western Colonialism in Asia, Africa and South Africa, the disintegration of Soviet Union and the emergence of USA as a single dominant power in the world.

The other land mark in Public Administration after Woodrow Wilson's article of 1887 was the 'Americanization[1] of Public Administration in Philippines, Korea, Japan, Thailand, etc. This was achieved through American Technical Assistance via USAID through some selected American Universities—such as University of Michigan, Indiana University, Syracuse University, University of Minnesota, University of Southern California and Ford Foundation.

It was not merely these American Universities but also some prominent American Scholars who were invited by Governments of the countries liberated from European colonial powers, which in a way resulted in the Americanization of Public Administration as a discipline. Some of the prominent American scholars in this category are Edward Litchfield and Alan Rankin of Cornel University (University of Indonesia); Paul Appleby (Indian Institute of Public Administration); John Montgomery and Milton Esman (faculty of Economics and Administration, University of Malaya). Other Departments of Public Administration were set up with the assistance of US Educational Foundation in Tribhuvan University, Nepal, etc. Other eminent University Professors from America to serve in the University of Philippines were Fred Riggs (Indiana University) and Prof. Egbert Wengert from Oregon University.

In spite of all these efforts Americanization of Public Administration in the Asian Region remained incomplete according to Prof. Carino for three reasons:

First, although little indigenous theory was revived or introduced, the practice of politics and administration remained at variance with the prevailing theoretical analyses and tools. The unease this situation caused generated the desire for 'domestication' of the discipline.

Second, the influence of other colonial masters persisted. The institutions established in Vietnam, Cambodia (now Kampuchea) and Laos, for instance, owed much to the assistance and example of France's Ecole Nationale d'Administration. Great Britain continued to attract citizens of its former colonies to its shores. There also seems to have been a greater exchange of professors and students among Commonwealth nations. Thus in Bangladesh, the faculty sport degrees from India, Lebanon, Malaysia, Australia and Canada. Or, in India, the first national seminar on the teaching of Public Administration was attended by two British professors.

Third, the enthusiasm for technical assistance for Public Administration seems to have burnt out by the beginning of the 1970's. This coincided with the demise of the Comparative Administration Group, the leader in the propagation of both technical assistance and development administration (Siffin, 1976). Perhaps both of these were brought about by the confluence of factors operating in the larger national and international context; the inability of growth to produce the aspired-for welfare and justice in the new states, the demystification of America with the failures of its War on Poverty and against Vietnam, and the disenchantment it reaped by its support of authoritarian governments in many states of the Third World. Out of these and the increased sense of efficacy among academics, their greater involvement in national crises, and the re-flowering of nationalism, there emerged a palpable movement in universities. This was marked by a thirst for, and appreciation of, critical thought and the search for native understandings and contributions to the field that could better describe, analyse, and uplift the teaching and practice of Public Administration in their own countries.

New Public Administration

During the 1970s the earlier concern of Public Administration with efficiency and productivity give rise to a new concern which was reflected in the Minnowbrook conference (Marini, 1971) resulting in a whole series of literature labelled as New Public Administration. A serious efforts was made by Vincent Ostrom to switch the predominant paradigm in the study of American Public Administration from a top down weberian bureaucratic approach to a 'democratic administration' bottom up approach based on (a) decentralised, fragmented authority (b) diverse, overlapping jurisdiction with Veto power in (c) public choice among competing delivering systems (Ostrom, 1973). Ostrom was also echoing the concerns of the New Public Administration Movement that American Public Organisations should better reflect the values and position of the whole society not just those of the power elite, that they should promote social justice in equity and that relations between them and their clients should be closer and softer (Caiden).

It is interesting to note that while the NPM movement gathered ground with a follow up conference a decade later by the participants of the 1st Minnowbrook conference, there was no attempt on the part of the public administratist in the 3rd world to introduce this concept and concern for the deprived sections of the population so far as the administrative systems and procedures were concerned. We can say that the grounds for NPM witnessed in USA were not the same as those in the underdeveloped countries of Asia and Africa.

We see the same anomaly in another field of Public

Administration called Development Administration. A whole new branch of discipline developed in America (Sverdlow, Siffin, Montgomary, etc.) called Development Administration. Prof. Corino (1991) mentions that while the United States exported 'Development Administration' but did not have it in its own shores. Instead it moved from traditional to New Public Administration, discipline not having to face issues of how to build and sustain a nation, how to handle racial and ethnic tensions, how to produce growth from the ravages of war and revolution, how to manage social change and how to concretise equity and justice. It is interesting to note that USA was trying to teach the 3rd world how to administer itself with ideas, concepts and tools that had not been used for handling the most ticklish problems of the value it was preaching, which was 'development'.

It would be but proper to summarise some of the important elements of Public Administration as it was transplanted in the Asian Region.

1. The discipline of Public Administration focused on the internal organisation as relations with the external environment were regarded as functions to be dealt with by the politicians.
2. Public Administration developed as a technical field, focused on methods even though these were yet to be proved effective, (e.g. O&M, policy analysis, etc.)
3. The 'Institution Building' became a major goal, not only in terms of creating units for the study but also for the practice of administration itself. The organisational mechanism for the job became equated with 'bureaucracy' large-scale rational and stable. This ignored the possible resort to and study of models more amenable to peoples participation and traditional way of doing things. Thus Public Administration seemed to advocate Government that was remote, formal and inaccessible. Its stress on hierarchy, unity of command

and top down leadership made consensus building, negotiations and other "Political Modes of Public Administration less explore", and authoritarian forms and political systems more acceptable supposedly only an extension of the efficiency and rationality of Public Administration itself.

4. The discipline was more attuned to urban problems but the methods and practice as applicable to US Urban Administration were not relevant so much for the towns and cities in Asian Region. It was even less applicable and realistic for the greater part of largely Rural Asia.
5. The contrast in the situation of new States with the presumed politico-social environment of the field was even more stark. Economy and efficiency may be appropriate criteria under conditions of regularity and stability, where processes of governance are on going and unquestioned. However, when communications facilities are non-existence and many areas inaccessible, a Government may have enough to do just by trying to maintain an adequate and effective presence. The bureaucracies of developing countries had first to promote the idea of territorial integrity and nationhood the questions posing them were how to administrator equity and justice, and how to provide peace freedom and security, subjects rarely mentioned in the American text books on Public Administration.
6. Value problems are so difficult to handle, not only because of the socio-geographic focus of the field, but also because Public Administration embraces logical-positivism which enshrined value neutrality and empiricism.

This resulted in a relative neglect of the role of values in administration.

New Public Management

It is difficult to pin-point at what stage and under what circumstances the ideas of Public Management as a paradigm in Public Administration started. One can safely say that it was a result of varying factors; some national, some international, political, economically and philosophically affecting various nations. While earlier paradigms of Public Administration reflected a dominant role of the Government (bureaucracy) in providing services hierarchical structure of organisations and centralisation, the New Public Management seeks to offer more efficient mechanism for delivering goods and services and for raising governmental performance levels (Kelly, 1998). One may like to note the starting point from the changes in administrative systems and procedures brought in as a consequence of the steps taken in UK by the Government of Margaret Thatcher in the 1980's. Traditionally many of the functions earlier performed by variety of Government and services where sought to be transferred to private institutions and organisations. This was the period when major public utilities in UK like Power, Energy and Coal were denationalised. Many ideas behind the NPM maybe attributed to the directives policies and programmes dictated by the World Bank and IMF to countries seeking their assistance. Since 1980's New Public Management has emerged as an important idea in mostly the Angle Section World (U.K., Australia and New Zealand). Naturally NPM has been defined in a variety of ways. Some of the definitions are quoted below:

"An inter-disciplinary study generic aspects of administration...a blend of the planning, organising, and controlling functions of management with the management of human, financial, physical, information and political resources (Garson and Overman, 1983)."

"A normative conceptualisation of Public Administration consisting of several inter-related components: providing high quality services that citizens value; increasing the autonomy of public managers, rewarding organisation and individuals on the basis of whether they meet demanding performance targets; making available the human and technological resources that managers need to perform well and appreciative of the virtues of competition, and maintaining an open minded attitude about which public performances should be performed by the private sector, rather than a public sector (S. Borins, 1995)."

New Public Management reminds me of the story of five blind men in a Village Mela having the feel of an elephant by touching the various parts of his body and having five different ideas. According to Professor Mohammed Ehsan (Administrative Change, 2004) 'NPM is different in many ways from traditional Public Administration'. Despite its tremendous appeal, traditional Public Administration all over the world failed to take cognizance of some vital environmental forces. Accordingly, NPM emerge in response to a number of environmental forces which governments everywhere have faced in the last twenty years.

First, large and expensive public sectors put pressures to cut programmes and/or increase efficiency.

Second, there have been massive technological innovations over the years, particularly the development of Information Technology.

Third, the globalisation of economy with increasing competition has become order of the day.

Fourth, it has become inevitable to liberalise the economic sector following heavy burden being imposed upon the national exchequer as a result of mismanagement, corruption, inefficiency in resource management, bureaucratic bungling, etc. More importantly increasing efficiency in resource management is also expected as economic recession and competition simply demand it.

Fifth, in the competitive world the people are demanding quality goods and services. They are now keen to compare services of all organisations (Borins, 1995; Minocue 1998; Hughes, 1998).

Prof. Ehsan mentions that the NPM model has several incarnations such as managerialism. New Public Management, market based Public Administration, and entrepreneurial Government, the basic premises are the same. Whichever model, one looks at, one thing is clear that NPM represents a major shift from the conventional Public Administration in various ways.

Several questions arise as to the feasibility of introducing this approach or thought that there can be a market based Public Administration approach. Can market-life practice be adopted to make administration efficient as well as responsive. What are problems likely to arise in an effort to move away from bureaucratic Government towards an entrepreneurial Government. Chief aim of market based public administration approach is that public administration can achieve its historic quest for both efficiency and responsiveness to the public through competitive market-like practices.

Recently I have come across some articles which indicate that New Zealand is the only country where they have introduced NPM as a major instrument of administrative reform. To some extent Australia is also adopting it.

The relevant question for us remains whether New Public Management is another name for bringing in market driven economy by making Government also market driven. It is not just a question of changing labels. Adoption of NPM will imply not only administrative changes and reforms but also a paradigm shift from the role of Government, the relationship between politicians and administrators, the abilities and qualities required for civil servants, the method of their selection, the accountability factor and so on. Perhaps it may even be necessary to bring about constitutional changes. New problems will arise; political, legal and constitutional. Our earlier experience shows that many of these new found slogans and labels borrowed from the West (whether USA or UK) does not solve our administrative problems. There is no harm in accepting the fact that there are areas which need to be conducted in a more business like manner by being more efficient and result oriented and not process oriented. These areas will have to be defined keeping in view the nature of the Indian society; the predominant rural nature of the society; the interest of the vast multitudes of people still living in dire poverty. The Prime Minister recently said we have still to tackle the basic problems of Agriculture, Health and Education. We will have to wait and see to what extent administrative reforms can be adopted so that new forms and methods of organisations structure involving non-governmental agencies may be evolved to tackle these basic problems and whether business houses will make substantial investments in these areas.

9

Ethical Concerns in Public Administration

RAMESH K. ARORA

'Ethics' is a system of accepted beliefs, mores and values which control human behaviour. More specifically, it is a system based on morals. Thus, ethics is the study of what is morally right, and what is not. The Latin origin of the word 'ethics' is *ethicus* that means character. Since the early seventeenth century, 'ethics" has been accepted as the science of morals; the rules of conduct, the science of human duty. Hence, in common parlance, ethics is treated as moral principles that govern a person's or group's behaviour. It includes both the science of the good and the nature of the right.

The ethical concerns of governance have been underscored widely in Indian scriptures and other treatises such as *Ramayana, Mahabharata, Bhagvat, Gita, Buddha, Charita,* by (Ashwa Ghosh), *Arthashastra*. *Panchatantra,*(Vishnu Sharma), *Manusmriti, Kural* (Thiru Valluvar), *Shukra Niti Kadambari* (Vana Bhatta), *Raja Tarangani* (Kalhan). *Hitopadesh* (Narayan Pandit).

One cannot ignore the maxims on governance provided by the Chinese philosopher such as Lao Tse, Confucius and Mencius.

In the Western philosophy, there are three eminent schools of ethics. The first, inspired by Aristotle, holds that virtues (such as justice, charity, and generosity) are dispositions to act in ways that benefit the possessor of these virtues and the society of which he is a part. The second, subscribed to mainly by Kant, makes the concept of duty central to morality: human beings are bound, from a knowledge of their duty as rational beings, to obey the categorical imperative to respect other rational beings with whom he interacts. The third is the utilitarian view point that asserts that the guiding principle of conduct should be the greatest happiness (or benefit) of the greatest number[1]. The Western thought is full of ethical guidelines to rulers, whether in a monarchy or a democracy. These concerns are found in the writings of Plato, Aristotle, Thoman Jefferson, Alexander Hamilton, Thomas Penn, John Stuart Mill, Edmund Burke, Disraeli and others.

The gist of wisdom on administrative ethics is that the public administrators are the 'guardians' of the administrative state. Hence, they are expected to honour public trust and not violate it. Two crucial questions raised in this context are "why should guardian be guarded?" and "who guards the guardian?"[2] (Rosenbloom and Kravchuk 2004: 516). The administrators need to be guarded against their tendency to misconceive public interest, promote self-interest, indulge in corruption and cause subversion of national interest. And they need to be guarded by the external institutions such as judiciary, legislature, the political executive the media and the civil society organizations. These various modes of control become instruments of accountability.

Ethical Concerns in Administrative Theory

It is essential to recognize that the discipline of Public Administration has been broadly influenced in the initial stages of its growth, by Political Science and the science of Management. While the philosophical premises of Public Administration were influenced primarily by Political Science, its technological facet was designed by Management Sciences. The early Political Science was taught as Moral Philosophy and Political Economy, while its current curriculum is the products of secular, practical, empirical and 'scientific' tendencies of the past century. The American students of Political Science, in the early years of the last century, were dismayed at the inadequacies of the ethical approach in the Gilded Age. Their interaction with the German universities and by virtue of the influence on their thinking by scholars such as J.N. Burgess, E.J. James, A.B. Hart, A.L. Lovell, and F.J. Goodnow, sought to recreate Political Science as a true science. They became increasingly interested in observing and analyzing 'actual governments'. Natural and Social Sciences substantially influenced their ideas and approaches. Later, Logical Positivism of the Austrian School influenced scholars such as Herbert Simon and thus there emerged a booming faith in developing a Science of Politics and a Science of Administration that would be able to 'predict and control' political and administrative life. As Dwight Waldo comments, the old belief that good government was the government of moral men was thus replaced by a morality that was irrelevant and that proper institutions and expert personnel were the determining factors in shaping good government. "The new amorality became almost a request for professional respect".

The eminence of behaviouralism until the mid-nineteen sixties further marginalized the ethical issues in the studies of Political Science and Public Administration. It was only after the advent of post-behaviouralism in Political Science and of New Public Administration, the scientific methods of behaviouralism and humanistic (read ethical) values struck a homogenous chord and the dispute between facts and values was resolved finally.

The current discipline of Public Administration accords value to 'values' of equity, justice, humanism, human rights, gender equality and compassion. The movement of good governance, initiated by the World Bank in 1992, lays stress, *inter alia*, on the ethical and moral conduct of administrators. While the New Public Management movement is more concerned with administrative effectiveness, the New Public Administration focuses on administrative ethics in its broader manifestation. Both the movements are destined to co-exist. This is as much true today as it was a hundred years ago when the industrial world was experiencing the rise of Scientific Management and amides a strong acceptance of the notion of administrative responsibility. John Kennedy, during his Presidency (1961-1963) had averred: "No responsibility of government is more fundamental than the responsibility of maintaining the higher standards of ethical behaviour.

The Bureaucratic Theory

The ideal-type construction of bureaucracy, propounded by Max Weber also highlighted an ethical imperative of bureaucratic behaviour. Weber observed:

In the rational type it is a matter of principle that the members of the administrative staff should be completely separated from ownership of the means of production and administration. Officials, employees and workers attached to the administrative staff do not themselves own the non-human means of production and administration.... These exists, furthermore, in principle complete separation of property belonging to the organization, which is controlled within the sphere of office, and the personal property of the official, which is available for his own private uses.[4]

Weber's analysis underscores the need to prevent the misuse of an official position for personal gains. Although his ideal-type construct on bureaucracy is not empirical, yet it has an empirical flavour for it appears to have taken into account the existential reality of bureaucratic behaviour. From a normative angle—knowing that Weber was not normative in his ideal type constructs—also, the message is clear: Don't misuse official property for personal benefit.

Most critics of real-world bureaucracies, including Harold Laski, Carl Friedrich, Victor Thompson and Warren Bennis, have criticized bureaucrats for violating the prescribed norms of moral conduct. Even Fred Riggs, while discussing the traits of a prismatic society like 'formalism' and 'nepotism' points out the yawning gap between the 'ideal' and the 'real' in administrative behaviour. The deviations from the norms and mores have been too glaring to be ignored. Immoral behaviour thus has become an integral component of 'bureau-pathology'.

The Environmental Context

Ethics, whether in an entire society, or in a social sub-system, evolves over a long period of time and is influenced, during its nurturance and growth, by a variety of environmental factors. Administrative ethics is no different. It is the product of several contextual structures and it never ceases to grow and transform. Let's look at some of these contextual factors that influence ethics in public administrative systems.

Historical Context: The history of a country marks a great influence on the ethical character of the governance system. The spoils system in the USA during the initial phase of the American nation vitiated the ethical milieu of the American public administration. "To victor belong the spoils" asserted the American President Jackson. Things would have continued the same way had not a disgruntled job-seeker not assassinated President Garfield in 1881. Garfield's assassination spurred the process of civil service reforms in the USA and the setting up of the US Civil Service Commission in 1883 was the first major step in this direction.

India has witnessed a long history of unethical practices in the governance system. Kautilya's *Arthashastra* mentions a variety of corrupt practices in which the administrators of those times indulged themselves. The Mughal empire and the Indian princely rule were also afflicted with the corrupt practices of the courtiers and administrative functionaries, with *bakashish* being one of accepted means of selling and buying favours. The East India Company too had a few employees who were criticized even by the British parliamentarians for being corrupt.

The forces of probity and immorality co-exist in all phases of human history. Which forces are stronger depends upon the support these get from the prime actors of politic-administrative system. What is disturbing is that a long legacy of unethical practices in governance is likely to enhance the tolerance level for administrative immorality.

In most developing nations having a colonial history, the chasm between the people and the government continues to be wide. In the colonial era, the legitimacy of the governance was not accepted willingly by a majority of population and therefore, true loyalty to the rulers was a rare phenomenon. Although the distance between the governing elite and the citizens has been reduced substantially in the transformed democratic regimes, yet the affinity and trust between the two has not been total even in the new dispensation. Unfortunately, even the ruling elite does not seem to have imbibed the spirit of emotional unity with the citizens. The legacy of competitive collaboration between the people and the administrators continues to exist. The nature of this relationship has an adverse impact on administrative ethics.

The Socio-Cultural Context

What values permeate the social order in a society determine the nature of governance system. The Indian society today seem to prefer wealth over any other value. And in process of generating wealth, the means-ends debate has been sidelined. Unfortunately, ends have gained supremacy and the means do not command an equal respect. A quest for wealth in itself is not bad. In fact, it is a mark of civilizational progress. What is important is the means employed while being engaged in this quest.

We seem to be living in an economic or commercial society where uni-dimensional growth of individuals seem to be accepted and even valued, where ends have been subdued by means, and ideals have been submerged under the weight of more practical concerns of economic progress. Can we change this social order? Mahatma Gandhi very much wanted to transform the priority-order of the Indian society, but there were hardly any takers or backers of his radical thinking steeped in a strong moral order. To put it bluntly, ever since Gandhi passed away, there has been not a single strong voice in independent India challenging the supremacy of Mammon. Neither our family values have questioned this unlinear growth of human beings nor has our educational system made serious efforts to inject morality into the impressionable minds of our youth. We have starkly failed on these fronts. The need is to evolve fresh perspectives on what kind of the Indian man or women we wish to evolve and how? Till then, efforts will have to be focused on the non-social fronts.

The issues of morality may or may not be rooted in the religious ethos a society. Indian religious and scriptures do not favour pursuit of wealth through foul means. Interestingly, Thiru Valluvar's *Kural,* written two thousand years ago in Tamil Nadu, emphasizes that earning wealth brings fame, respect and an opportunity to help and serve others, but it should be earned through right means only.

The level of integrity among Protestants and Parsees is supposed to be relatively higher when compared to other religious and one can find the roots of such integrity in the well-ingrained mores of these religions. Nevertheless, there are several secular groups as well which are known for their high moral conduct.

The cultural system of a country, including its religious orientation, appears to have played a significant role in influencing the work ethics of its people. For instance, the stress on hard work, so characteristic of the Protestant ethics, has helped several Christian societies to enhance their per capita productivity. While Judaism has valued performance of physical labour by its followers, in Hindu and Islamic societies, on the other hand have generally considered physical labour of a lower ranking than does the mental work.

The family system and the educational system are influential instruments of socialization and training of the mind in its impressionable years. In case the values inculcated through the family and the school have underscored honesty and ethics, the impact on the mind-set of citizens is likely to be highly positive and powerful.

Legal-judicial Context

The legal system of a country determines considerably the efficacy of the ethical concerns in governance system. A neatly formulated law, with a clear stress on the norms of fair conduct and honesty, is likely to distinguish chaff from grain in the ethical universe. Conversely, nebulous laws, with confusing definition of corruption and its explanations, will only promote corruption for it would not be able to instill the fear of God or fear of law among those violating the laws of the land and mores of society. Besides, an efficient and effective judiciary with fast-track justice system will prove a roadblock to morality in public affairs. Conversely, a slow-moving judiciary, with a concern for letter rather than the spirit of the law, will dither and delay and even help the perpetrators of crimes by giving them leeway through prolonged trials and benefits of doubts.

Likewise, the anti-corruption machinery of the government, with its tangled web of complex procedures, unintendedly grants relief to the accused who are indirectly assisted by dilatory and knotty procedures.

In India, there is hardly and effective anti-corruption institution. Lok Pal has yet to be established, Lok Ayuktas are feeble and toothless agencies, while the state vigilance bodies are low-key actors. The consequences are too obvious to warrant any explanation.

The Political Context

The political leadership, whether in power or outside the power-domain, is perhaps the single most potent influence on the mores and values of citizens. The rulers do rule the minds, but in a democracy particularly, all political parties, pressure groups and the media also influence the orientation and attitudes on moral questions. If politicians act as authentic examples of integrity, as happens in the Scandinavian countries, or as examples of gross self-interest, as found in most South Asian countries, the administrative system cannot remain immune from the levels of political morality.

The election system in India is considered to be the biggest propeller to political corruption. Spending millions on the elections 'compels' a candidate to reimburse his expenses through fair or foul means—more foul than fair. While fair has limits, foul has none.

It is generally argued that the administrative class—comprising civil servants at higher, middle as well as lower levels—emerges from the society itself. Naturally, therefore, the mores, values and behavioural patterns prevalent in the society are likely to be reflected in the conduct of administrators. To expect that the administrators will be insulated from the orientations and norms evidenced in society, would be grossly unrealistic.

The above argument has a convincing logic, yet there can be a counter-point that the rulers are expected to possess stronger moral fibre than do the subjects. Since there are hardly any instrumentalities to protect and nurture administrative morality vis-a-vis the general social morality, such an expectation remains at the most an elusive ideal. Hence, there is an obvious need to go deeper into the problem.

The behaviour of politicians has a demonstration effect on civil servants. Besides, the capacity of the less honest political masters to control civil servants is immense. It is ironical that the moral environment in a country like India is designed more by its politicians than by any other social group. The primacy of the political over the rest of systems is too obvious to be ignored.

In case the media is objective and fearless, its role in preventing corruption can be effective. It can even act as a catalyst to the promotion of ethical behaviour among administrators. Hence, those who own and manage the media should understand their wider social and moral responsibility.

The Economic System

The level of economic development of a country is likely to have a positive correlation with the level of ethics in the governance system. Even when a causal relation between the two is not envisaged, a correlation cannot be ruled out. A lower level of economic development, when accompanied with inequalities in the economic order, is likely to create a chasm among social classes and groups. The less privileged or more deprived sections of society may get tempted to forsake principles of honest conduct while fulfilling their basic needs of existence and security. Not that the rich will necessarily be more honest (though they can afford to be so), yet what is apprehended is that the poor while making a living may find it a compelling necessity to compromise with the principles of integrity.

It is Interesting to note that with the advent of liberalizing economic regime in developing nations, there is a growing concern for following the norms of integrity in industry, trade, management and the governance system on account of the international pressures for higher level of integrity in the WTO regime. This is what Fred Riggs would call 'exogenous' inducements to administrative change.

FOCI and Concerns

An important question arises in connection with the moral obligation of an administrative system? Is the administrative system confined to acting morally in its conduct or does it also share the responsibility of protecting and promoting an ethical order in the larger society? While most of the focus on administrative morality is on the aspect of probity within the administrative system, there is need to consider the issue of the responsibility of the governance system (of which the administrative system is an integral part) to create and sustain an ethical ambience in the socio-economic system that would nurture and protect the basic moral values. Moral political philosophy assumes that the rulers will not only be moral themselves but would also be the guardians of morality in a society. Truly, being moral is a prerequisite to being a guardian of wider morality. Both the obligations are intertwined.

It is a truism that the crux of administrative morality is ethical decision-making. The questions of facts and question of values cannot be separated from ethical decision-making. Thus the science of administration gets integrated with the ethics of administration. And in this integrated regime, only that empirical concern is valued which respects the normative concerns in the delivery of administrative services.

Which are the essential concerns in regard to administrative ethics? There can be a long list of values that are considered desirable in an administrative action. However, in being selective, one has to focus on the most crucial values.

Let us then concentrate on the value of justice, fairness and objectivity. Woodrow Wilson, the Princeton scholar who broached the issues of ethics in his seminal article "The Study of Administration" (1887), when he became the U.S. President and delivered his inaugural address in 1913 averred that justice was more important than sympathy. Thus, he placed justice at the top of value-hierarchy in a governance system. Paradoxically, there has been a lot of discussion on the formal-legal aspects of administrative law, since then, but very little analysis has been made of the philosophical dimension of administrative justice.

The other two issues of ethical decision-making, viz. fairness and objectivity are in fact integral components of administrative justice. When administrators are true to their profession, they are expected to be impartial, and fair and not be influenced by nepotism, favourtism and greed while making decisions of governance. Objectivity should not be misconstrued as a mechanical and rigid adherence to laws and rules of decision-making angle. It has undoubtedly wider ramifications encompassing a set of positive orientations.

Currently, the notion of ethics has expanded itself to involve all major realms of human existence. Let us attempt the salient aspects of ethics in public administration. Broadly, it could summarized as following maxims:

1. *Maxim of Legality and Rationality:* An administrator will follow the law and rules that are framed to govern and guide various categories of policies and decisions.
2. *Maxim of Responsibility and Accountability*: An administrator would not hesitate to accept responsibility for his decision and actions. He would hold himself morally responsible for his actions and for the use of his discretion while making decisions. Moreover, he would be willing to be held accountable to higher authorities of governance and even to the people who are the ultimate beneficiaries of his decisions and actions.
3. *Maxim of Work-Commitment*: An administrator would be committed to his duties and perform his work with involvement, intelligence and dexterity. As Swami Vivekanand observed: "Every duty is holy and devotion to duty is the highest form of worship". This would also entail a respect for time, punctuality and fulfillment of promises made. Work is considered not as a burden but as an opportunity to serve and constructively contribute to society.
4. *Maxim of Excellence:* An administrator would ensure the highest standards of quality in administrative decisions and action and would not compromise with standards because of convenience or complacency. In a competitive international environment, an administrative system should faithfully adhere to the imperatives of Total Quality Management.

5. *Maxim of Fusion*: An administrator would rationally bring about a fusion of individual, organizational and social goals to help evolve a unison of ideals and imbibe in his behaviour a commitment to such fusion. In situation of conflicting goals, a concern for ethics should govern the choices made.
6. *Maxim of Responsiveness and Resilience:* An administrator would respond effectively to the demands and challenges from the external as well as internal environment of which the administrative system is a part. He would adapt to environmental transformations and yet sustain the ethical norms of conduct. In situations of deviation from the prescribed ethical norms, the administrative system would show resilience and bounce back into the accepted ethical mould at the earliest opportunity.
7. *Maxim of Utilitarianism*: While making and implementing policies and decisions, an administrator will ensure that these lead to the greatest good (happiness, benefits) of the greatest number.
8. *Maxim of Compassion*: An administrator without violating the prescribed laws and rules, would demonstrate compassion for the poor, the disabled and the weak while using his discretion in making decisions. At least he would not grant any benefits to the stronger section of society only because they are strong and would not deny the due consideration to the weak, despite their weakness.
9. *Maxim of National Interest*: Though universalistic in orientation and liberal in outlook, a civil servant, while performing his duties, would keep in view the impact of his action on his nation's strength and prestige. The Japanese, the Koreans, the Germans and the Chinese citizens (including civil servants), while performing their official roles, have at the back of their mind a concern and respect for their nation. This automatically raises the level of service rendered and the products delivered.

10. *Maxim of Justice*: Those responsible for formulation and execution of policies and decisions of governance, would ensure that respect is shown to the principles of equality, equity, fairness, impartiality and objectivity and no special favours are doled out on the criteria of status, position, power, class, caste or wealth.
11. *Maxim of Transparency*: An administrator will make decisions and implement them in a transparent manner so that those affected by the decisions and those who wish to evaluate their rationale, will be able to understand the reasons behind such decisions and the sources of information on which these decisions are made.
12. *Maxim of Integrity*: An administrator would undertake an administrative action on the basis of honesty and not use his power, position and discretion to serve his personal interest and the illegitimate interests of other individual or groups.

There could be many more tenets added to the above catalogue of maxims of morality in administration. However, the overall objective is to ensure 'good governance' with a prime concern for ethical principles, practices, orientations and behaviour. There are no dogmas Involved in defining administrative ethics. The chief concern while doing so is the positive consequences of administrative action and not just ostensibly rational modes of administrative processes.

In the following pages, a few of the salient concerns and foci are being dealt with briefly.

Code of Ethics

The concept of ethics has been a late-comer in the realm of public administration. For too long, doing one's duty well was considered to be equivalent of bureaucratic ethics. Interestingly, the original city managers' and federal code of ethics placed notable stress on efficiency as ethical concept. In the early twentieth century, the perspective began to change. In 1924, the International City/Country Management Association adopted the public sectors first code of ethics that reflected anti-corruption and anti-politics facets of the municipal reforms movement.

In 1958, the US Congress imposed a code of ethics on the Federal Government and in 1978, founded the Office of Government Ethics as an upshot of the Ethics in Government Act of 1978. In 1992, the Office of Government Ethics released the Federal Government's first comprehensive set of standards of ethical conduct, comprising standards pertaining to gifts, conflicts of financial interest, impartiality misuse of office, seeking outside employment, and outside activities. Almost all the American states have also promulgated their respected codes of ethics, though compared to the federal initiative, there are less comprehensive.

Today, codes of ethics, ethics boards, and ethics training have been accepted as integral aspects of public administration in the US. Moreover, ethics education has also permeated the discipline of Public Administration. The National Association of Schools of Public Affairs and Public Administration has made ethics education as a required component of a public administration programme for its accreditation and has prescribed that all introductory text books in Public Administration should include a discussion on ethics (Browman, Berman and West 2001.). Eminent professional associations of public administration also offer training programmes on ethical conduct for public managers.

In India, there are a few training programmes on administrative ethics offered by the Indian Institute of Public Administration and other institutions, but there is hardly any similar initiative taken of in the realm of education in Public Administration.

The American Society for Public Administration had adopted in 1984 a Code of Ethics for its members (comprising intellectuals as well as practicing administrators). It was revised in 1994. Certain salient points of the ASPA's Code of Ethics are as follows.

- Exercise discretionary authority to promote public interest.
- Recognize and support the public's right to know the public business.
  Exercise compassion, benevolence, fairness and optimism.
- Prevent all forms of mismanagement of public funds by establishing and maintaining strong fiscal and managements controls, by supporting audits and investigative activities.
- Protect constitutional principles of equality, fairness, representativeness, responsiveness and due process in protecting citizen's rights.
- Maintain truthfulness and honesty and to not compromise them for advancement, honour, or personal gain.
- Zealously guard against conflict of interest or its appearance: e.g. nepotism, improper outside employment, misuse of public resources or the acceptance of gifts.
- Establish procedures that promote ethical behaviour and hold individuals and organizations accountable for their conduct.

There are several other 'commitments' include is the ASPA's Code of Ethics. The document can serve as a model for various public employee organizations in India and other countries to draft and follow similar codes of ethics. In fact, it would be ideal if all public administrative agencies—ministries, departments, boards, commissions, public enterprises, urban administrative authorities, rural administrative organizations and other public institutions—adopt and honour such codes of ethics, allowing minor variations in view of the specific nature of their functional areas and organizational requirement. The whole thing has to turn into a movement which will take some time to muster popular acceptance and credence.

In this context, Alka Dhameja points out, even though no ethical code can provide answer for every decisional dilemma, yet such a code can provide guidelines while dealing with critical moral paradoxes in administrative decisions and actions.[5] Surely, it may not be possible to draft comprehensive or exhaustive ethical codes for administrative decision-making, yet efforts can be made to make them as inclusive as possible. More importantly, such codes should be drawn up by the administrators themselves and not imposed from above. These have to strike a balance between what is ideal and what is possible. Extremities are generally resisted in the empirical word of human affairs.

Dhameja rightly suggests that the conduct rules should not be confined to the don'ts of administrative behaviour but should also be helpful in resolving ethical dilemmas. Cases and illustrations can be helpful in guiding administrators in complex decisional situations. However, no conduct rules can be absolutely specific. Certainly generalities will always enter the drafting of such rules. But what is of important is scan and scrutinize them at regular intervals and modify them in tune with the changing social imperatives, revised economic parameters and the prevailing cultural milieu. A code that is impractical or archaic is rarely honoured in practice. We are not advocating laxity in the enforcement of codes of ethics, but only highlighting the essentiality of 'realism' while defining morality. A judicial blend of 'ought' and 'possible' will make an ethical code a helpful instrument in sustaining an ethical order.

Work Ethics

An important dimensions of ethics in Public Administration is work ethics. It represents a commitment to the fulfillment of one's official responsibilities with a spirit of dedication involvement and sincerity. It also implies that a government functionary would love his work and not treat it as a burden or a load. And that efficiency, productivity and punctuality will be the hallmarks of his administrative behaviour.

Efficiency has been a constant concern of administrative analysis and good governance. The notion, transcending the classical school, has permeated the New Public Management philosophy. Efficiency implies doing one's best in one's job, with a concern for maximum possible utilization of human, material and financial resources and even time to achieve the prescribed and desired objectives.

Let us give a fresh look at the notion of efficiency. Can we treat efficiency as 'ethics'? Truly yes, for a genuinely efficient person has a regard for the higher goals of governance, including public welfare and he devotes himself to the expeditious achievement of those goals. Thus an 'efficient person is also an ethical person. He possesses administrative morality that is basically rooted in a conviction in the desirability of ethical conduct. Here we are not equating efficiency with mechanical productivity but with higher levels of performance that juxtaposes the ideal with the applied facets of organizational function.

This raises another question. Why is that the quality of services and goods produced by the government organizations is relatively poorer than that normally observed in non-government sector? Government schools, government dispensaries and government officers provide an unsatisfactory look and render dissatisfactory services. In fact, the overall work culture in public systems in India is relatively lower than that prevailing in the public sector and that existing in the government systems in most developing countries. Even when we compare India with China, South Korea and Japan, we have staggeringly low per capital productivity. The answer might lie in systemic flaws—poor infrastructure, sloppy monitoring, lackluster control and evaluation and almost an absence of reward and punishment system. Yet the major factor behind the poor quality of output of public systems is the carelessness and callousness on the part of government functionaries. Most of them do not have a feeling of 'oneness' with their organization and their job. They do not put up their best in their work and are half-hearted in their involvement in duties. Resultantly, there are unrealistic policies, irrational decisions, erratic changes in government systems and an indifference towards the beneficiaries of the system. All this may not be illegal, yet it is grossly immoral. In rendering public service, sometimes even being amoral is being immoral.

Once we agree that work ethics is important to organizational morality and once we accept that sound time management and a respect for punctuality and promptness (as against procrastination) in work disposal is a valued attribute, we should device strategies for improving work ethics in developing countries including India.

A few corrective steps may be considered in this context. There should be prescribed specific norms of productivity and work performance for organizational units and even individuals. A 360° performance appraisal system should be adopted. This would be feasible only if job descriptive and role and responsibilities of each position are specified. There should be maximum delegation of powers at every level with a concurrent system of effective monitoring and work audit. Punctuality and promptness in administrative affairs must be valued and along with the quality of work performed, these should become criteria for reward and punishment in organizations. The seniors should lead by example. They should motivate their juniors to take initiative, responsibility, and be enterprising and efficient. Conversely, those suffering from indolence, indecision, inefficiency and dishonesty should be punished. This would set an example and create a healthy work culture by those who conduct the public business. The same spirit pervades the pronouncements of public leaders at the helm of governments in most nations. Thus, ethics has regained its status as a distinctive characteristic of good government and the discipline that studies it. The trend is not likely to reverse in the foreseeable future.

Hopefully, there would be a greater concern for quality in public affairs and public service, and the movement of Total Quality Management (TQM) will pervade the functioning and influence the performance of government structure. Ethics means good service and this maxim applies most to public systems.

Empathy and Compassion

Public administration is designed to serve 'public'. By its very nature, it ought to be people-oriented and even people-centered. While bureaucracies are expected to be guided by laws and rules, it is not necessary to make them mechanistically rule-centric. Public administrative organizations are human organizations and they ought to be humane in their policies, decisions and orientation. Being responsive to people's needs enjoins upon civil servants to be responsive to their psychological needs of being cared for, nurtured, and helped. It is in this context administrators ought to evolve and demonstrate a higher level of emotional intelligence and spiritual intelligence that would make them 'feel' for the common man and simultaneously respect his feelings.

Despite all the visible prosperity in India, one cannot ignore massive deplorable poverty in India. As a long as there is a single poor person in this country, the moral responsibility of administration remains to help the poor. But the larger issue of empathy and compassion is not confined to demonstrating positive behaviour towards the less-privileged sections of society. It transcends this orientation. In fact, anyone having access to administration should be meted out a treatment of respect. This treatment should not be just ostensible, but be real, authentic and profound. Ethical behaviour emanates from a pure and kind heart, and therefore, those who are in the business of serving people should train their heart to be sensitive and compassionate.

Compassion involves a sense of empathy. It does not end

with pity. It invokes sensibilities to understand and even feel the pain of others and propels one to be truly helpful to overcome this pain. Hence, administrative ethics in public affairs envisages that the domain of feelings and the universe of rationality will have a happy blending in the thought and action of civil servants.

A positive and healthy approach to services entails courtesy and politeness in administrative behaviour, a desire to help resolve their problems, satisfy them even when on account of legal constraints, extra help cannot be rendered and matters have to be disposed off in accordance with the legal and formal requirements of the system. A citizen-centric administration would be strengthened through such an attitude.

Two areas where administrators ought to show an attentive and caring attitude is to provide correct and useful information to clients when they need it and to redress satisfactorily the citizens' grievances. Even when a grievance cannot be redressed, at least a citizen expects an explanation as to why it cannot it be redressed. What is important is a positive approach to dealing with people and being helpful to them and not avoiding them or considering them as burdensome. Ethics entails a respectful attitude to the citizens.

Right to Information

Fostering 'Sunshine' in public administration is one of the best methods of ensuring higher standards of administrative ethics. Openness is the enemy of corruption. Almost all countries of the world have Freedom of Information or Right to Information Acts. In the U.S. at the federal level, freedom of information and open hearings provisions are integral part of the Administrative Procedure Act. In India, the Freedom of Information Act of 2002 has been redesigned as Right to Information Act which is likely to be enacted in 2005. Besides, a number of state governments including Goa, Rajasthan, Tamil Nadu and Maharashtra have enacted legislations that help in securing accountability of public employees through this device.

Legislation, however, is not enough. Its enforcement would require a will on the part of the state, a willingness on the part of administrators and an initiative coupled with courage on the part of citizens themselves. The state machinery should ready to punish those civil servants who obstruct the implementation of Right to Information Act. The age-old orientation to treat every information as 'secret' must give way to greater openness. This would require a transformation of the mind-set of administrators. Large-scale to reorient the thinking of administration at all level, more particularly at the cutting edge level.

The movement for the Right to Information cannot succeed unless people themselves become motivated to ask for the fructification of this right. People's groups, such as the one led by Aruna Roy, will have to take initiative at a massive scale. Even the educational system will need to play a purposive role in this realm.

Whistle-blowing

In the American system, whistle-blowing by public employees is considered as legitimate and statutorily protected. Public employees are expected to use their voice to protest administrative activities that are illegal or immoral. They can even resort to resignations from their positions to give vent to their protest. And these acts are considered moral and appropriate.

In the American federal government, there functions a hotline, called Fraud Net, which for preventing fraud, waste and abuse. Through this hotline, employees and others can anonymously report instances of misconduct for investigation to the General Accounting Office. Besides, the American public employees enjoy constitutional protection on speaking out on matters of public concern like dangers to public health or safety.

In Britain, a new appeals procedure for civil servants has come into effect. Under this procedure, a civil servant could raise concerns, confidentially, with an individual outside his normal hierarchy. When he believes that the response is not satisfactory or reasonable, he may report the matter to the Civil Service Commissioner.

The Constitutional Review Commission in India considered the possibility of whistle-blowing as a statutory activity, but it was not accepted as a viable choice. The need is to develop a fresh perspective on this issue.

Obstacles to Ensuring Ethical Accountability

David Rosenbook and Robert S. Kravchuk raise a question: Why is it difficult to guard the guardians? (2005: 526529). There are certain intrinsic features of the administrative system that make it difficult for the external regulating institutions to control and to ensure its accountability. A few of these imponderables are discussed here.

Special Expertise and Information

Public administrators are often experts in their specific area of functioning and it is difficult for any outside agency to surpass them in their areas of specialization. Moreover, they generate and control crucial information that may be difficult to be accessed or even comprehended by law regulators, much less by the common citizen. Although the Right to Information Acts (or similar legislations) are there in most countries, there is cost to be paid for obtaining information and verifying its authenticity. The administrators do not easily part with such information and are too keen to let their citadels remain impregnable.

Full-time Status

Most public administration are full-time, while outsiders cannot devote equal amount of time in overseeing their activities—legislators, judiciary, Comptroller and Auditor General of India and even the media have relatively less time to keep a watch over the actions of administrators. They cannot seek all the crucial information from administrators and even if they get it, they do not have sufficient time to process and use it effectively.

Massive Expansion of Bureaucracy

In a country such as India, the role of public administration has been increasing incessantly. Its regulatory, developmental, promotional and entrepreneurial responsibilities have been multiplying and with that its size. The number of public personnel as well as the agencies they work for have gone up so much that it is difficult for the political executive or the legislature to exercise effective control over them. Likewise, in large-sized organizations like Public Work Department, Income Tax Department, Police Department, etc., it is impossible for higher officials to keep an eye on the conduct of their subordinates. The geographical distributors of government agencies also makes the span of control too wide to be handled effectively. Even computerization of all personnel records cannot ensure a surveillance over the conducting all personnel.

Lack of Coordination

The number and kinds of agencies to ensure probity in public administration have also been increasing continually. In India, for instance the Central Bureau of Investigation, the Central Vigilance Commission, State Lok Ayuktas, State Vigilance bodies and Anti-Corruption Departments are co-existing without effective coordination among themselves. There are lacunae in working the vigilance machinery and absence of harmony among the various agencies. For years altogether, the permission to prosecute government officials is not granted to the Anti-Corruptions Department and very often such permission is denied. The national Lok Pal has yet to be appointed and there is no agency that is doing the job supposed to be undertaken by him. The Judiciary is slow and there are no fast-track courts for dealing with cases of corruption.

As mentioned already, in the United States, the Ethics in Government Act of 1978 created an office of Government Ethics (OGE) in the Office of Personnel Management. The Ethics Reforms Act of 1989 strengthened the OGE, now an independent agency within the executing branch. No such institution exists in India and in most developing countries.

Excessive Security

Most countries grant protection to civil servants and refrain from punishing them for the common lapses in the performance of their duties. Besides, there are no punishments prescribed for non-performance or for low productivity. Article 311 of the Indian Constitution makes it almost impossible civil servant. A sense of over-security pervades the personnel system and the inquiry system is so dilatory and cumbersome that it is devoid of any threat or fear. Resultantly, a low level of discipline in most government organizations. And when corruption permeates all the echelons of administrators in an organizations the potential efficacy of internal control becomes woefully meager.

Misinterpretation of Role and Obligation

Civil servants frequently engage themselves in actions that are unethical and against public interest. Over a period of time, they get used to defining their role and responsibilities in a parochial manner that is either self-centered, group-centered or organization-centred and not people-centred. Since all important professional groups, including the politician also adopt a tunnel-vision in perceiving social reality there are hardly any countervailing forces on the prevention or correction of a parochial interpretation of public interest by the administrative personnel. As a result, both ethics and accountability suffer.

There is a general tendency among administrators to view public interest from a narrow angle and tunnel vision. Their specialization and the specific goals of their organizations prompts them to focus on the achievement of narrow organizational goals. In this process, the issue of public interest may get submerged under organizational interest. The Excise Department of a State, for example, may be interested opening more wine and beer shops in order to earn more revenue and thus ignore the impact this expansion of sale network of intoxicants will have on the physical and moral health of citizens.

The political pressures imposed from above also colour the vision of administrators. Occasionally, one notices that the Police Department, because of pressure from its political bosses is caught between the compulsion of hierarchy and the obligation of duty. The police officials generally succumb to political pressures in order to save the interest of their own self and of their families. Occasionally, 'inconvenient' civil servants are punished with transfers to 'difficult' locations or postings that may cause problems to their families.

Orthodox Loyalty

In India and in most developing countries, public employees are socialized into developing loyalty towards the organization that they serve and to the superior authority under whom they work. It is customary in the Indian society to show respect to the superior and to refrain from criticism of one's boss and in the public organization. Any voice against the superiors is considered as an act of insubordination. In such a cultural climate, even the honest and conscientious employees do not speak out against unethical practices of their peers and seniors. And the undue compassion occasionally shown to the subordinates on their errors of omission and commission also tend to strengthen the 'soft state'. All this represents a misplaced loyalty and magnanimity that eats into the vitals of the ethical order in public administrative system.

As the Indian democracy becomes more mature, it is hoped that whistle-blowing will be considered a legitimate and rational activity and will be protected under the laws and rules.

Trivial and the Substantive Ethics

The conduct rules for civil servants emphasize on meticulously following the norms of good conduct. Some of these rules have remained unchanged since long and now appear to be ridiculous. No wonder, these are ignored by all.

Likewise, there is a stress that official property, equipment and stationery should not be used for personal purposes. These relate, *inter-alia* to the use of official vehicles and phone. Such rules are "conspicuous", more in their violation than in their enforcement[9] and compared to broader issues of ethics and morality, these are at best examples of trivial or petty morality. Not that they should be ignored but should not replace the more significant ethical concerns of duty, fairness, objectivity and commitment. In matters of administrative ethics, occasionally we tend to be 'penny wise and pound foolish'.

Employees' Unions

Another impediment in the way of enforcing discipline and codes of conduct is the tendency of employees unions to resist the managerial action against their members even when they have violated ethical norms. Assertive or aggressive unions can throttle any actions, even a legitimate one, against their members. As a result, the supervisory level leadership in public systems get exasperated and start ignoring the unethical actions of their subordinates. In a political system where employees unions are aligned with powerful political parties—whether in power or in opposition—administrative leadership refrains from taking a tough stand even against the culprit employees for fear of compulsive back-tracking or humiliation. It has been observed that collective bargaining agreements seriously jeopardize the managerial authority to discipline their employees. Occasionally, the courts also show greater consciousness about the protection of the so-called 'constitutional' rights of workers than of the citizens, irrespective of the ethical issues involved.

Corruption

Corruption is the abuse of officials authority for personal gains. It is betrayal of public trust for protecting private interests. Corruption is currently viewed a universal phenomenon, although the nature of quantum of corruption differs from nation to nation. The international and the national press in India are replete with instances of corruption in government. Politicians and administrators are generally in league with each other in perpetuating corruption. Citizens thus become the victims of immorality in governance. Little wonder, one finds in various nations terms in common use that denote the existence of corruption in cross-national settings. In the Middle East and in India, because of the Mughal influence, *baksheesh* is a tip that is used to seek the favours of an administrative functionary at the lower level. Its name changes to *dash* in Western Africa 'Speed money' in India implies a fee to expedite the processing of a government favour; *la mordida* or 'the bite' are popular forms of bribes in the Latin America; *shtraff* is the Russian version of a small bribe; *la bustarclla* cannotcs a little envelope (containing bribe) in Itality; while in Israel, '*protekzia*' refers to the exploitation of personal contracts to achieve a favourable treatment from administrators (Rosembloom and Kravchuk, 2005: 521). And in the United States—a country rated high on the integrity index of the Transparency International, one comes across strange term such as Watergate, Iran-Contragate, White-watergate and Filgate.

Unfortunately, the standards of ethics in the governance system have differed staggeringly in the proclamations and in practice. The Constitution, laws, policies, manifestoes of political parties and speeches of politician are replete with direct or indirect references to ethical basis of governance, but in practice, however, there is a gross violation of moral precepts in the functioning of the politico-administrative system.

The critical reasons behind administrative corruption are scarcity of what people want from public administrators and the inconveniences involved in the normal channels of administrative decisions. As Michael Johnston explains:

> The demand for government's rewards frequently exceeds the supply, and routine decision-making processes are lengthy, costly, and uncertain in their outcome. For these reasons, legally sanctioned decision-making processes constitute a 'bottleneck' between what people want and what they get. The temptation to get around the bottleneck—to speed things up and make favourable decisions more probable—is built into this relationship between government and society. To get around the bottleneck, one must use political influence—and corruption, which by definition cuts across established and legitimate processes, is a most effective form of influence. (Johnston 1982:3).

Because of the scarcity of what people want from the government, they are willing to pay bribes in exchange for jobs, land, licenses, quotas, admissions, passports, utility service connections etc. or for getting them speedily or illegitimately. They may also bribe administrators for escaping arrests, punishments, fines or a major inconveniences. All these are examples of a transactional corruption. This acquires frightening proportions when it becomes an accepted trait of the socio-cultural system.

President Dwight D. Eisenhower who was the American President from 1953 to 1961, had once warned his nation of the existence of a 'military-industrial complex' which promoted a culture of 'transactional corruption' based on *quid pro quo*. C. Wright Mills in his monumental work, *The Power Elite* (1956) had also broached the issue of such alliances and their impact on government decision-making. In India, B.B. Vohra, then Home Secretary of India, had presented in 1995, a report on the activities of crime syndicates/mafia organizations which had developed links with or were being protected by government functionaries and political personalities. The conclusions of the Vohra Committee reflect a moral crisis in the India governance system. Not that the decline is irreversible. Strong and honest efforts with indomitable will can sincerely halt the process of decline. Certain Asian countries have already proven that it is possible to combat and curb corruption. It requires effective political and administrative will to do so.

Almost all kinds of political systems are affected by administrative corruption. (Heidenheimier 1970). In totalitarian societies and military regimes, corruption might get concentrated at the higher echelons of party, military or civilian bureaucracy, while in democracies, it might spread throughout the system. In 'soft states' particularly, political as well as administrative corruption has greater potentiality of percolating the governance system. Weak control and supervisory mechanisms cannot prevent corruption and consequently, these become its catalysts.

In a civic culture or democratic society like India's, politicians who get elected on people's support and vote, are primarily concerned with strengthening their constituencies and thus are keen to dole out benefits to those who are their supporters. Administrators, on the other hand, more keen to follow the prescribed procedures. In situations of conflict between the politician and administrators, there is either a stalemate, or eventually, politicians win. But the most convenient course for politician is to win over administration to their side and make them partners or collaborators in corruption with the protective hands of politicians above them while with a temptation for gaining extra (illegitimate) benefits, administrators consciously align with their political masters and indulge in corruption. Very rarely, honest and strong administrators stand up who refuse to succumb to politicians pressures and cajoling and likewise, there may be a few politician who apply brakes to the bandwagon of administrative corruption.

There is witnessed a 'weather-cock' syndrome in relation of government corruption. When the top rung of the political or administrative executive gets tough on corruption, the middle and lower level hierarchy in both the system get cautious on the issues of ethics. Greed is curbed by fear but only as long as fear is genuinely feared.

Subversion

While corruption is endemic in government organization, there is another ethical blemish that afflicts, though rarely, the administrative system. Certain government servants, working in sensitive organizations like ordinance factories, atomic energy establishment and defence forces, may pass on critical secrets to enemies in exchange for pecuniary benefits or for the sale of extra-territorial loyalty. In contemporary times of global competition, even economic subversion is possible. There may be, within the government, attempt to subvert friendly relations with foreign countries. In extreme or ideological reasons, subvert certain government programmes like family planning or prevention of illegal migration. There can be many other cases involving ethical issues in public administration. Attempt should be made to devise strategies to combat them.

Accountability and Ethics

Accountability and ethics are closely related. Effective accountability helps the achievement of ethical standards in the governance system. Legislative or parliamentary control through questions, debates and committees provide ample opportunity to the people's representatives to raise among others issues of ethics and morality in the governance system. More particularly, the Public Accounts Committee in India which gives its comments on the report of the Comptroller and Auditor General of India in its reports raises matters that directly or indirectly relate to ethics and good governance.

In the USA, the Office of Government Ethics, an independent agency, helps the Senate in the process of confirming or rejecting presidential appointments, particularly in matter of financial decisions.

"Ethics can be considered a form of self-accountability, or an 'inner-check' on public administrators' conduct." (Rosenbloom and Kravchuk 2005: 516). Self-accountability and external accountability are interrelated for it is the latter that imposes expectations on the former. However, there are certain time-tested norms of moral conduct that determination the nature of self-accountability. These precepts of moral philosophy may considered as external checks. Essentially, however, it is the synthesis of external as well internal checks that determine the parameters of administrative ethics. The higher* the level of ethics, less the need for strong instruments of accountability and control. Conversely, lower the level of ethics, greater the need for potent means for ensuring accountability.

Max Weber had maintained that the outside (extra-agency) checks on public administration were inadequate. Hence, the value of self-accountability is immense. The desire to be ethical in one's profession should spring from within. Seventy years ago, John Gaus in his book. *The Frontiers of Public Administration* (1936) had remarked that public employees were expected to exercise an 'inner check' rooted in professional standards of administration and ideals.

New Public Management: Counter-View

The traditional public administration laid great emphasis on efficiency and economy. Likewise, conventional Management Science was greatly concerned with productivity and performance. The New Public Management, with its neo-Taylarian orientation, has focused almost exclusively on performance and results.

During Bill Clinton's presidency, Al Gore, the US Vice-President, advocated through the National Performance Review's (NPR) version of the NPM, that ethics implied achieving high degree of customer satisfaction. It believed that people—in government or out—were basically honest and well-intentioned and there was no need wasting time and energy on focusing on corruption. Trusting them is bound to lead to a favourable climate for ethical behaviour. The cost of deterring corruption is too high in terms of red tape such efforts crests. The NPR underscored that reinventing government required innovations which in turn implied deviations from the grooves of tradition. Distrusting and accusing people for their creative initiatives dampens their enthusiasm for innovation. Trusting the employees as well as the people they serve would help carve a more effective administrative system in the self-governing democracy (Gore 1993: 1995).

Al Gore seems to have transcended even Douglas McGregor's Theory Y and created an image of man who is creative and honest. Naturally, such a man in government would not need measures of external control over him for he has internalized very well the canon of self-accountability.

Even if we consider Al Gore's portrayal of a government personnel too idealistic, it has a lesson to offer. Should we not question our excessive concern with prevention of corruption and instead adopt a more balanced perspective on the issue of ethics. Does not an over-concern with corruption take our attention away from the more crucial issues of people's welfare through innovative measures and well-intentioned initiatives on the part of public employees? In other words, there are high costs of combating corruption that we should be conscious of. No doubt, such an awareness should not cause a laxity in tackling corruption. Instead, it should help appreciate the value of promoting greater trust in public system. Trust begets trust. Optimum vigilance is a requisite to the reinforcement of a climate of trust for they are complementary and mutually supportive.

It would appear that such an emphasis on trust and de-emphasis on control and would be more applicable to societies having a higher level of integrity and probity in public life than to those which have low standards of morality. Thus, there cannot be uniform approaches to talking corruption in the governance system. Much would depend upon the levels of morality and rectitude prevailing in a society.

Training

An important aspect of bureaucratic socialization is training. As is well known, there are three kinds of training that an administrator undergoes. Here we are not discussing pre-entry trainings such as provided in the professional educational stream. We are primarily concerned with training that is imparted and obtained after a person enters the administrative service. First is the induction training comprising foundational, institutional and field training organized soon after an administrator's career starts. The second is in-service training that is imparted throughout the service career in the form of refresher courses, orientation programmes, seminars and conferences. The third is on-the job training that is subtly provided by job performance and observation. What is paradoxical is that despite a great deal of talk on ethical aspect of administration, the stress on ethical training in the induction training as well in-service training is woefully meagre. There is a pervasive feeling in the administrative circles that morality cannot be taught through training. May be this true, may be it is not. There is no way to prove or disprove it, since no concretely organized research has gone into it.

We must not however abandon the option of ethical training and hence take rigorous initiative to make ethics as an integral and prominent part of induction as well as in-service training. Already, national and international training institutions have prepared modules on this theme. The need is to establish our faith in this kind of training and execute the idea with appropriate acumen and skill.

As for the on-the-job training the impact on the mind-set of a government functioning of the immediate work-environment around him is immense. Principled and honest superiors and members of the peer group are bound to invoke morality in the conduct of a government servant. Conversely, if the official ambience encourages ethical laxity and compromises, it becomes easier for the personnel to join the bandwagon of immorality. No wonder, certain departments such as Income Tax, Excise, Customs, Commercial Taxes, PWD and Police are infamous for their low ethical standards, for the countervailing and corrective forces therein are feeble.

Can this situation change? No doubt, it can. The will and the efforts, however, must match the challenge. This is a tall order, but not too formidable to be real. Many nations, whether Kamal Pasha's Turkey or contemporary South Korea have shown resilience to transform their bureaucratic order and its attendant mind-set. Other countries can also follow suit, and they must.

The Media

In an open society, media can play an important role in highlighting unethical practices in the governance system. The role that *Washington* Post played in exposing the Watergate Scandal in USA earned laurels from all sections of society. In India, *The Indian Express, The Hindu* and a few other newspapers have acted as active watchdogs over public affairs. Vernacular press has also acted responsibly in this respect. Recently, the sting operations by a few TV channels on the Commercial Taxes and Public Works Department in Delhi have also brought the issues of cutting edge level corruption to the center-stage. The best part is that the government, the legislature and even the judiciary do take notice of such reports and initiate action on most occasions. What is needed is a rigorous follow-up of the action taken on such revelations by the media itself.

Conclusion

When A.D. Gorwala presented his report on *Public Administration in India* in 1951, he had emphasized that integrity was one of the cardinal philosophical premises of good administration. It is paradoxical that despite visible decline of moral standards in public life, the mainstream reports on administrative reforms have not focused on ethical issues.

Except for the Santhanam Committee report on the Prevention of Corruption in India in 1964 and a specific segmented report on the theme, Railway Corruption Enquiry Committee by Acharya Kriplani in 1955, there have been no major efforts at recommending strategies for integrating moral values with the administrative system at various levels. True, the ARC report on Lok Pal and Lok Ayukta was published in 1966, but that again was confined to structural changes rather than on bringing about an new ethical order in public systems.

In 2005, with the announcement of the intention of appointing a second Administrative Reforms Commission by the Manmohan Singh government, ethical concerns of public services are likely to be accorded a respectable place in the emergent inquiry on administrative reforms in the country.

The need is to go beyond the general statements of administrative morality and be more meticulous in recommending modifications in laws, rules, structures and behavioural patterns in the specific context of individual departments or organizations. The issues of ethics in the Police Department, for instance, carries a distinctive character and possible solutions than, say, in the Education Department. This would further require a rigorous modification in the laws and procedures pertaining to specific functional areas.

How is the administrative ethics of the twenty-first century likely to be different from that of the twentieth century. The answer is to be found in the increasing convergence of ethical concerns at the cross-national level. Globalization of the economic order is likely to pave the way for the globalization of governance issues. Not that there would be universally uniform configurations of the governance system, much less the bureaucratic systems. But with the mitigation of chasm among nations in the realm of the goals, philosophy and strategies of governance, the ethical concerns are likely to transcend international boundaries. These will reflect the classical concerns of public administration like efficiency, responsibility, accountability and integrity along with the emergent beliefs in equity, justice, openness, compassion, altruism, responsiveness, human rights and human dignity. Hopefully, there would be discernible the blossoming of a new citizenship committed to the sustenance of administrative morality. Even for nurturing such a positive citizenship, public administration institution will have to act as facilitators and educators. That is the biggest challenge as well as an opportunity for the administrative system for times to come.

BIBLIOGRAPHY

Agarwal, U.C. (2000): "Administrative Corruption: Causes and Cure" in Noorjahan Bava, ed. *Public Policy and Administration: Normative Concerns.* New Delhi: UppaL.

Bowman, James S., Berman, Evan M. and West, Jonathan P. "The Profession of Public Administration: An Ethics Edge in Introductory Textbooks?" *PAR* 61 (March/April 2001), pp. 194-205.

Dhameja, Alka (2003): "Role of Ethics in Public Administration" in Arora, Ramesh K. and Saxena, Tanjul, eds, *Ethics and Accountability in Government and Business.* Jaipur: Aalekh.

Gore, Al. (1993): *From Red Tape to Results: Creating a Government that Works Better and Costs Less.* Washington D.C.: Government Printing Press.

Gore, Al. (1995): *Common Sense Government Works Better and Costs Less.* Washington: D.C.: Government Printing Press. Government of India, Ministry of Home Affairs. *Vohra Committee Report,* 1993.

Heidenheimier, Arnold J. *Political Corruption: Readings in Comparative Analysis.* New York: Holt.

Hobson, Archie (2002): *The Oxford Dictionary of Difficult Words.* New York: Oxford University Press.

http://www. gao. gov/fraudnet htm

Johnston, Michael (1982): *Political Corruption and Public Policy in America.* Montrery, Calif. Brooks/Cole.

McSwite, O.C. (1996): "Postmodernism, Public administration and the Public Interest" In Wamslay, Gary L and Wolf, James, F. eds. *Refounding Democratic Public Administration.* London: Sage.

Rohr, John A. (1978): *Ethics for Bureaucrats: An Essay on Law and Values.* New York: Marcel Dekker.

Rosenbloom, David H. and Kravchuk, Robert. S. (2005): *Public*

Administration Understanding Management, Politics and Law in the Public Sector. Sixth edition. New York: McGraw-Hill.

Stone, Donald C. (1983): 'Foreword' to Kenneth Kerrangan and O.P. Dwivedi, eds. *Ethics in Public Service Comparative Perspectives.* Brussels: HAS. Quoted in Bava, Noorjahan (2004): "Ethics in Public Life" in Sanjeev Reddy, P.L. *et al., Pursuit of Institutional Excellence: Essays in Honour of V.K.N. Menon.* New Delhi: IIPA.

Waldo, Dwight (1984): *The Administrative State* Second edition. New York: Holmes and Meier Publisher.

Weber, Max (1947): "The Essentials of Bureaucratic Organization: An Ideal Type Construct." In *The Theory of Social and Economic Organization* (Trans. A.M. Henderson and Talcott Parsons, ed. Talcott Parsons).

10

New Public Management and the Developing Societies

SRINIBAS PATHI

Throughout the world today, there is a movement that envisages change and development with the help of good governance'. While some critics argue that 'good governance has been a part and parcel of the core issues of public administration through ages, the World Bank and a number of US think tanks have been instrumental in putting it on the international agenda at present. It stands for an ideal condition or a conceptual framework that has roots in the international political economy. It is often dubbed as one of the dominant post colonial paradigms. Its thrust areas include, among others, strategic and result-oriented mechanisms that is efficient, effective and qualitative; decentralisation of administration coupled with the empowered structures of urban and rural local government; alternative provisions for public services and utilities such as privatization of energy distribution, house keeping, sanitation and security service etc; explicit performance contracting including work-based and task-based contracts; competitive work environment within and between public service organisations such as electricity distribution companies; greater accountability and transparency through the mechanisms like Right to Information and Citizens' Charters;

alternative systems and methods of public finance and budgeting such as service-wise budgeting based on actual performance and appraisal; elimination of corruption and corrupt practices and strengthening of the citizen's grievance redressal system such consumer grievance redressal fora and commissions; improvement of the system of service delivery at the cutting-edge administration; new and innovative work culture and responsive or citizen-friendly administration; and, last but not the least, new public management or adoption of the best practices of the private sector.

Here, we come across the notion of New Public Management (NPM). Before analysing the meaning, nature, background, key areas of concern, major gaps and related issues of NPM vis-à-vis the developing societies, it is pertinent to discuss an innovative idea called 'a new standard for the governance of public services' as being practised in the United Kingdom. The persons who serve on the governing bodies of the public sector organisations would have a single common standard, just like, the combined code of the private sector, that clarifies expectations of their roles and responsibilities. According to an estimate by the British Treasury, public expenditure in the UK will exceed 500 billion pound sterling by 2005-06 financial year. Effective governance and financial management would be essential if this money is to achieve the quality of services and value for the members of the public along with the expectations of the tax payers.

The 'standard of good governance' has been developed in UK by the Independent Commission on Good Governance in Public Services. It prescribes guidance to review, challenge and question governance practice and to seek improvements. The Commission believes that the standard will help the public functionaries to review their own efforts and to make sure that they receive the support they require to perform a difficult task effectively. The public regulators can use the standard to assess the accountability of public service organisations on the basis of performance, demand changes and patterns of improvement in service delivery. The standard presents six core principles such as, first, a focus on organisation's purpose and outcomes for citizens and service users; second, effective performance of activities in relation to clearly defined functions and roles; third, promotion of values for the whole organisation and demonstration of the same through behaviour; fourth, adoption of informed and transparent decisions and effective management of crisis; fifth, development of the capacity and capability of the public service providers; and, finally, engagement of the stakeholders and making the process of accountability real.

In the backdrop of good governance paradigm, let us discuss the core issues relating to New Public Management (NPM). To begin with, it is the political economy of public management reform. It entails the new forms of economic decentralisation and adjustment along with their implications for policy design and regulation. It revolves around the notions of public-private partnerships; effective and efficient management of public finance and aid-allocation. It also involves new thinking and ideas on the design of a well organised regulatory frame-work. But it is pertinent to analyse the NPM vis-à-vis the specific socio-political and economic systems like the developed or the developing societies. Perhaps this is the single-most important reason behind NPM's varying degrees of success in different societies.

Queries are often raised as to the relationship between public administration and public management. While public administration is basically concerned with the activities of the Government carried out by the Ministries, Departments and such other Agencies; public management primarily deals with the functions and activities concerning public goods and services. For instance, in the Indian context, the core of public management may be traced to the supply of electricity, public transport, telecom, insurance, banking, health care services etc. These sectors employ a large chunk of the organised labour and involve huge public investments. Most of these services are categorised as infrastructure services which play a vital role in the organisation and optimization of economic development and. progress. In public management, it is not the 'public' element comprising administrators, administrative theories and administrative apparatus like public policies that apparatus like public policies that dominates; but it is the 'management' element covering people, beneficiaries, participants, stake holders, goods, prices, investment, returns, quality etc. which is at the centre stage. Outwardly, it may seem that the ultimate responsibility of service provisions rest with the Government. But there is ample scope for developing and promoting public-private cooperation for achieving the best possible results to the advantage of the common people. Here, we may refer to the on-going telecom revolution in India. On 20th April, 2005, all the telecom players in India—both in the public and private sectors—met in a telecom conference. Dayavindhi Maran, Minister, IT and Communication, Govt. of India, urged the private sector telecom companies to emulate the practice of BSNL, the public sector company in the matter of 'roaming charges' on mobile phones. And just hours after the said meeting, a number of major private sector telecom companies announced thirty-three percent cut in their roaming charges.

There are a number of key areas concerning New Public Management. To begin with, there is the notion of E-governance. It stands for Information Technology (IT) driven system that is used to make administration efficient and effective. It makes us of computer, networks, internet and other related techniques with a view to providing prompt, timely and cost effective services. E-governance often stands for SMART (Simple, Minimal, Accountable, Responsible, Transparent) governance. It makes use of information and communication technology to reinvent the political economy and to reform public administration. Its salient features include information sharing, pro-active services, open methods and better service delivery at different levels of government. In a developing society like India, both the central government and a number of state governments have embarked upon the E-governance project. But there exist a number of problem areas such as computer literacy, internet connectivity, lack of inter-departmental coordination, gaps in E-governance planning, monitoring and evaluating the output.

It may be pointed out that creating and sustaining an open and transparent government is a pertinent questions before all the societies in the world today. It has been viewed widely by the practitioner and critics alike that transparency and accountability in public administration can be ensured by a vibrant civil society backed by well-designed constitutional and legal frame-work as well as easy and free access to information. The stake-holders in particular and the people in general should be allowed to participate in the public decision-making process with the help of effective and timely exchange of ideas, information and view points. Such steps and initiatives contribute positively to the growth of trust in government. While strengthening the civic capacity of public institutions and authorities, they also try to fulfil some of the genuine requirements and demands of the civil society.

Another key area is 'outsourcing'. Today, governments try to minimize costs and maximize output by way of utilising services of private players as partners. As an integral part of the New Public Management discourse, public systems and public bureaucracies acknowledge the ever-growing importance of networked forms of administration as against the traditional hierarchical structure of public administration. Such a situation has its far-reaching implications pertaining to the distinction between 'administrators and managers'; 'national, provincial and local governments'; and 'public and private sector'. Here, the main thrust is on the issues like achievement of policy objectives; provision of quality public services; and scope for effective people's participation.

There is a link between the emerging financial market and New Public Management. In this context, a number of issues, activities and processes require a special mention that include, among others, macro-level international cooperation and partnership initiative like Foreign Direct Investment (FDI) in hither to core sectors of the national economy; mobilisation of the small investors and micro-management of local finance and related resources; an understanding of the dynamics of capital market operations and adoption of appropriate measures to withstand emergencies; adoption of a more liberal and pragmatic attitude towards the concepts like income, compensation, interest, cost, dividend etc.; creation of and awareness about consumer rights and duties; a forward looking approach towards the issues relating to research and development initiatives etc.

Traditionally, the governmental organisations including the public enterprises had the supply orientation. It means that they were concerned with their supply of goods and services irrespective of the needs of the people. But under NPM, there is a change over to demand orientation which means that the needs and aspirations of the people determine the nature of goods and services and not vice-versa. Adhocrism in public systems must be replaced by proper planning, implementation strategies, monitoring and mechanism for feedback.

New Public Management is a trend that has received acceptability in the United States and oilier Western Societies. In all these societies, direct role of the government in many sprees receding which are increasingly being taken over by the private players. And the governmental agencies make use of various tools like contracts, grants, vouchers and loans to get their work done. In such cases, the MNCs, national private agencies, local subsidiaries and networks of agencies and private groups collaborate at various levels to perform the designated or assigned tasks and functions.

New Public Management makes extensive use of internal competition, i.e., both within the public system mechanism and between public and private players. This is closely related to the notion of market competition. So, some of the proponents regard it as the new institutional economics. It involves networking and aggregation of public authorities like the bureaucracies; greater competition through contracting out;

and wider choice for the stake-holders and consumers. But serious doubt are now being raised regarding the nature and strength of the private players in most of the developing societies which in turn give rise to numerous questions regarding the efficacy of NPM principles and practices in such societies. Second, in the absence of credible national private players in such societies, MNCs their subsidiaries and such other outside forces enter into these societies which creates more problems and predicaments. The national governments almost become handicapped in dealing with these foreign agencies. The factors like constitutional norms, statutes, administrative regulations and practices are seldom acceptable to the outsiders. There are other vital issues like labour laws, environmental sustainability, cultural tradition and even national sovereignty which are not addressed in proper perspective. In many cases, the governmental agencies are required to share some of their basic functions with the private parties, national or international or multinational, which include among others, power of direction, control over public finance; spending of public money; and utilisation of vital public resources like land, air, water, forest, mines, oceanic wealth etc.

As part of the NPM trend, flexibility and excessive transparency lead to chaos and confusion. Everybody's responsibility actually means nobody's responsibility. It becomes difficult to fix responsibility and accountability. In the developing societies, where poverty, illiteracy and lack of awareness among the bulk of the population determine the nature of socio-economic and political order, the private players, either internal or external, can't be given a free hand. There is much talk about the role of the hidden hand of private capital or market forces in the political process of the developing societies. But this situation would be completely out of control when such forces will be positioned in the actual driver's seat of the political economy in such societies.

Market is a reality. But it can never be our total universe. The economic factors might determine the nature and pattern of our living process. 'But they are definitely interwoven with other political, social, cultural, moral and intellectual factors. Thus, mindless application of NPM strategies and practices in the developing societies would lead to disastrous consequences.

BIBLIOGRAPHY

1. Maurean Mackintosh, Rothin Roy, eds., *Economic Decentralisation and Public Management Reforms,* Chettenham: Edward Elgar, 1999.
2. B.N. Ghosh, *From Market Failure to Government Failure: A Handbook of Public Sector Economics*, London: Wisdom House Publications, 2002.
3. Atul Kohli, ed., *The Success of India's Democracy,* Princeton: Princeton University Press, 2001.
4. V.S. Naipaul, *India. A Million Mutinies Now,* London: Heinemann, 1990.
5. R.K. Mishra, 'Delivering Effective Education and Training for Public Administration Reforms: A Case Study', *Indian Journal of Public Administration,* New Delhi: IIPA, No. 2, 2002.
6. Lawrence Harrison, Samuel Huntington, eds., *Culture Matters: How Values Shape Human Progress*, New York: Basic Books, 2001.
7. Litvack, Lennie, Admand, Junaid *et al., Rethinking Decentralisation in Developing Countries,* Washington DC: World Bank, 1998.
8. Robert K. Merton, *Social Theory and Social Structure,* New York: The Free Press, 1968.
9. L.M. Salamon, *The Tools of Government: A Guide to the New Governance,* Oxford: Oxford University Press, 2002.
10. Elliott D. Sclar, *You Don't Always Get What You Pay For: The Economics of Privatisation,* New York: Carnell University Press, 2002.
11. Michael Barzelay, *The New Public Management: Improving Research and Policy Dialogue*, California: University of California Press, 2001.
12. Stefanie Teggemann, 'Corruption, Poverty and Inequality', Washington DC: World Bank, 2002; also see www.worldbank.org/publicsector.

II

New Public Management

V. BHASKARA RAO

About sixty percent of countries in the civilized world irrespective of their ideology, (social, economic and political) and levels of development have been under reform process particularly during the last 30 years. The role of the state and government in these countries came under attack to a large extent due to certain historical situations, emerged during this period.

1. Failure of 'Big Government' and welfare state;
2. Downfall of socialist governments in some countries;
3. End of Cold War between capitalist and socialist states;
4. Virtual bankruptcy of developing countries and mixed economies;
5. Poor performance of public bureaucracy in all countries;
6. Emergence Neo-Liberalism, Managerialism and Market domination;
7. Emergence of Globalisation forces;
8. Demand for democratization and decentralization; and
9. Pressure of international institutions and agencies.

In order to meet this unprecedented historic situation, in the context of liberalization and globalisation the states and governments in most countries have been called to restructure their administrative organizations for improving government performance.

The nature and scope of this study is limited to a discussion about various strategies adopted by most governments around the world for the successful introduction of administrative reforms.

The current reforms are aimed at a major change in the ideals[1] and practices[2] of traditional civil service. The assumption is that administrative reforms are needed everywhere and that they will bring benefits. The reform efforts are deliberate and designed towards a desired change.

Reform Strategies adopted by different Countries

Name of the country	*Reform Strategy*
Australia	Financial Management Improvement Programme, Reforming the Australian Public Service.
Austria	Administrative Management Project
Canada	Public Service-2000
Denmark	Modernization Programme for the Public Sector
France	Renewal of the Public Service
Japan	Fundamental Policy of Administrative Reform
Portugal	Major options' plans
UK	Financial Management Initiative, Next Steps and Citizens Charter
Netherlands	Towards More Result Oriented Management
Norway	Plan for the Readjustment of Central Government Administration in 1990's
Spain	Reflections on Modernization of the Public Administrations
USA	Creating a Government that works Better and Costs Less
Malaysia	The Quality Revolution and The Malaysia Incorporated
New Zealand	Economic Management
Belgium	State Modernization and Computerization of Public Services Secretariat.
India	Action Plan for an Effective and Responsive Government

Administrative reforms enjoyed significant support in Europe, USA, Australia and New Zealand during 1990s. They permeated Latin America, entered Asia and very recently penetrated Africa[3]. These reforms have been manifested in different ways and at numerous levels.

Two institutions—unaccountable Big Business and indifferent Big Government—caused most concerned[4] to the society. There is universal unhappiness with the administrative system. Public institutions created long back failed to keep abreast with the times. In response to the fall from public grace[5], since the mid-1980's there has been a common trend in many of the industrialized countries to redefine the role of the state and public administration in society. Several international bodies such as the International Monetary Fund, the World Bank, the Commonwealth and the United Nations commissioned studies and recommended a number of strategies[6] for administrative reform. Their agenda include[7]:

"Liberalization, deregulation, downsizing the public sector, shrinking bloated public organizations, privatization, debureaucratisation, civil service reform, budget reform, performance measures, business like management, long-term transparency, computerization, and mechanization, and greater productivity, efficiency and accountability".

The agenda had many targets, including government as an economic manager and the role of government in society. The civil service was singled out for criticism. It was accused of many things—of being bloated, expensive, unresponsive, deliberately resistant to changes and incapable of dealing with new challenges. In short, the civil service lacked the ability to concentrate on clients and manage operations efficiently and to provide sound and unbiased policy advice. The civil service was thought to sabotage new programmes, to undermine attempts at major policy and administrative reforms. Hence, the fundamental task of administrative reformer is to regain control of the public sector and greater control of the broad public policy agenda. The politicians made it clear as they wanted doers not thinkers. They felt that they themselves had the policy answers. Officials understood the message clearly and developed a tendency to recommend safe policy options and what 'politicians would wear'. As such virtually the senior civil service has been the target of administrative reform.[8]

Political Will and Commitment

"Failure to understand the political nature of administrative reform and to develop a political strategy to overcome resistance lies behind the failure of many reform attempts"[9] The prerequisites of reform include political will and a strategy of implementation. The study of politics cannot be overlooked in analyses of administrative reform.

Administrative reforms of the 1980s and 90s can be considered essentially a deliberate attempt to use power (political) and authority to influence the changes of goals, structure and processes of state bureaucracy.

At the outset, the reforms seem to be wide ranging, involving a major shake-up in administrative organizations to remedy the malfunctioning of traditional processes. But, in its in-depth analysis, it reveals the dominance of neo-liberal economics over politics, i.e., the state and the governance. Therefore, it is necessary this time to understand the nature and extent of reforms in proper perspective. The intensity of change is indeed more political and economic and less administrative. The strongest political impulse for every phase of administrative reform came from the 'new right', while defenders of the old order had themselves been weakened and divided.[10]

The new right criticized the existing old order at least on seven counts.[11]

1. The state in dealing with the powerful interest groups (especially trade unions) resulted in higher public spending than the median voter would have supported.

2. Public officials were mainly concerned with the maximization of their own budgets and status.
3. The professions were regarded as self-interested monopolists, restricting the supply of their services, demanding higher salaries and pursuing their own professional ends rather than responding to users of their services.
4. The growth of government undermined the freedom of the individual.
5. 'Big Government' sapped the entrepreneurial spirit of the citizen and the sense of self-reliance.
6. Centre-Left governments mistakenly pursued artificially egalitarian notions of social justice, which undermined the individual freedom and the fiscal self-discipline of the state.
7. The expansion of the public sector had stunted private sector growth.

The conservative governments of the 1980s and 90s repeatedly expressed their anti-state stand[12]. Different anti-state theories were fed to the political masters in different countries through a "variety of right wing think-tanks" and influenced the policy formulation. Their advises appeared to be more pragmatic to the situation rather than appearing to be based on any particular anti-state theory.

In the past despite the intellectual attacks and public criticism, against the maladies of the public bureaucracy, ruling political parties and their leaders never seriously condemned the bureaucracy. But, now it is well known that the leading politicians in US, UK, Canada, Australia, New Zealand and other countries have been openly hostile to state bureaucracy. "Bureaucratic bashing', by political leaders has become a common tactic to denigrate public employees and generate public support and win elections[13].

The present assault on the public services justified radical pro-market reforms, in downsizing the public sector, transforming the public service on the lines of business enterprise it facilitated the expansion of political control over public bureaucracy[14] and enabled them[15] to introduce reforms emulating the techniques used in the business sector.

It is argued that two swings upward from national governments to international organizations and downward from national governments to grass-roots non-governmental organizations—are the keys to understanding the changes that confront public administration in the 1990s.[16]

It is debated that the manifestations of globalisation have an impact on administrative reform: such as:

Reinventing government. Deregulation, the shift in decision-making powder to sub-national levels of government (devolution) is a consequence of globalisation, increased inequality (higher unemployment and lower wages for workers is a consequence of globalisation, its concern is to bring changes in governance and not just government.

Reinventing Government

Osborne and Gaebler through their book[17] popularized the term 'Reinventing Government' they raised issues that confront state administration and developed "entrepreneurial government with a ten point programme:

Empowering citizens, promoting competition between providers of goods and services, promoting mission driven leadership in order to street rather than row", decentralizing authority, measuring outcomes, earning money, deregulation, preferring market mechanisms, performance budgeting, support for civil service reform and catalyzing all sectors—public, private, voluntary.

The features of the book caught the attention of anti-bureaucracy campaigners. They were welcomed as the characteristics of a new form of public management.

By the mid-1990s, some states in US were actively implementing the "reinvention" reforms particularly the components of total quality management[18]. Thought, Reinventing Government has received wide publicity and prestigious political endorsement, it appears to be "more of a ripple than a reform wave at the state level.[19] The reforms urged under the 'reinvention' banner are not widely and quickly adopted across the state.

Managerialist Reforms

The core reform ideas and principles included in most national efforts of the past 20 years are frequently lumped under the term managerialism[20]. In general terms, the new set of techniques and practices of calculation and control reliance on competition to ensure quality, customer orientation etc. collectively represent managerialism. The reform introduced in the public service as a part of managerialism is better known as New Public Management (NPM). The NPM reforms are more complex[21].

Terms such as 'search for excellence', 'Quality management', 'public sector productivity', 'organizational well-performing', 'entrepreneurial government' are also used along side the dominating label of NPM. NPM embraces almost similar reform strategies and concepts[22]. NPM's typical aim is to provide cheaper services to customers and citizens responding to their demands by supplying more value for money, freedom of choice, flexibility and transparency[23]. It focuses on performance. It invites managers to accept responsibility for the whole system.

The concept of NPM is derived from the ideas of New Institutional Economics (NIE), i.e. the theory of Public Choice and the business-type Managerial Movement[24]. NPM as a movement attempts to bring a more economic rationality in public administration. NPM is based upon the ideas of neo-conservative liberal economic policy, particularly the NIE.

Thus, it may be considered apolitical-ideological movement. However, it is important to note, not only conservative governments in UK and US, but Labour Governments in Australia[25] and New Zealand also implemented the NPM reforms. It means NPM offered a frame-work which suits the needs of every one. It claims to be politically neutral and provides an apolitical frame work enabling to pursue different values and functions within multiple political priorities.

NPM has been presented as a remedy to cure management ills in various organizational contexts. Through, the concept of NPM still suffers from serious deficits some countries like Britain, Germany, USA, Canada and New Zealand implemented NPM. NPM is mainly oriented towards the 'internal running of public organizations, where the role of public manager as a leader is important[26]. NPM always takes place within an institutional, political and administrative context[27]. It is not a monolythic administrative reform doctrine.

The 'new paradigm'[28] called the NPM has several interrelated components":

1. High quality of services that citizens value-customers expect.
   UK's citizens' charter launched by John Major, the Prime Minister in 1991, provides global statement of the government's service quality commitments. Singapore has set-up a service improvement board in the Prime Minister's office to keep a watch on departmental efforts.
2. Increased autonomy to the managers, in U.K, Australia, New Zealand and Singapore, the operating responsibilities of the Central Departments are shifted to specific agencies with clear performance targets and increased autonomy. More powers in financial and personnel management are devolved to the local managers. Organizational structures are being simplified and hierarchies flattened to create conditions for development of more positive and productive managerial leadership.
3. Rigorous performance measurement of individuals and

organizations have been periodically reviewed in Canada, Australia and UK. Pay structures are based on fulfillment of performance targets. In UK and New Zealand Tenure System is being replaced by fixed term contracts. The public agencies are asked to be more cost-conscious and resource-saving.

4. To achieve the pre-set performance targets managerial support services are facilitated in the shape of human and technological resources like human resource management, information technology. Australia developed and implemented affirmative action plans for women, migrants, aboriginals and the disabled, expecting expansion of the pool of new talent available to the government.
5. NPM advocates receptiveness to competition and an open-minded attitude by the public sector. Private sector and non-governmental organizations are invited to involve themselves in social, economic activities that were formally reserved to the public sector. Privatization has been adopted as an official policy in most of the nations that have undertaken administrative reforms (UK privatized about 47 services since 1979). Public-private joint-ventures are also encouraged in some countries avoiding the rigidity of the 'public sphere'.

Policies supporting the private sector activities have been adopted, such as dismantling price controls, deregulation and downsizing the public sector. It seems that the neoclassical economics has almost-captured the public sector all over the world. Therefore, it is feared that the new paradigm of NPM may as well lead to hijacking of the state by the 'private' and 'powerful' interests.

However, the orientation of NPM reform depends on the role and types of the states[29] and the shape reforms occurred. NPM cannot offer 'universalist' solutions. The government capacity to perform new roles is a serious constraint on the effective implementation of NPM[30]. Thus, all the components of NPM are underpinned by a rethinking of the role of government, characterized as a move from a concern to do towards a concern to ensure that things are done?[31]. The experience of six countries which are known for the NPM reforms shows little evidence of a trend towards managerialism[32]. Non-motive goals of managerialist or NPM theory cannot be realised at least within the existing political systems, unless 'the rules of the game' are modified, with the following six principles[33]:

1. Separation of policy from operation
2. Clear definition of contracts between agency and ministers.
3. Sufficient operational authority.
4. Rigorous performance measurements.
5. Maintenance of accountability and structures.
6. Independence of civil service.

Contracting Out/Privatization

Over the past two decades, many services previously provided by government agencies (public utilities) have been taken over by the private sector. In many countries government business enterprises (public sector) have been privatized and government funding of services either has been maintained or reduced (Disinvestment), or the provision of services has been contracted out. It is assumed that this experiment is taking place on the division of functions as 'Core' and 'Non-Core' functions. It raises the key question about the role of the state.

The core roles of the government needs to undertake are assumed as, stronger role in policy-making, coordinating other actors, regulating, facilitating and providing information. In the 'non-core' sector privatization, autonomous non-governmental, public organizations including contracting out is permitted. These assumptions implied development of a 'capable state' but a 'minimal' role for government[34].

It is claimed that contraction of the role of government is an inevitable reaction to the developments in the global economy. But it may not be beneficial. For, it not only dismantles the policies of the mixed economy and welfare state but restores the situation prevailing 100 years back in Laissez Faire State. The most important cause for this situation is because of the loss of confidence in the capacity of governments to control the economy implying a greater need to cultivate "business confidence'[35].

Privatizing[36] and down sizing government institutions began by Margaret Thatcher in UK. Her government published a revolutionary document in February 1988, "Improving Management in Government: The Next Steps". The purpose of Next Step[37] proposals was to transform the delivery of the vast majority of central government services by establishing departmental executive agencies—where the productivity and effectiveness could be more easily measured and monitored. The Chief Executives of these agencies were brought from outside the government to create a new management culture. By 1995, over 100 Next Steps agencies were created and nearly two-thirds of the British Civil Service was employed in those agencies. The Chief Executive Officers of the Agencies report directly to the ministers concerned.

Creation of Next Steps agencies is considered a compromise between market and traditional forms of organization. They were seen as alternative to privatization or an incremental step towards privatization. Though two-thirds of the British Civil Service operates on the Next Steps lines the programme of public sector reform appears to be relatively modest and restrained when compared to the radical and comprehensive reforms in New Zealand[38]. The reforms in New Zealand, were first initiated by the Labour Government (1984-1990) and subsequently pursued by Liberal Conservative Government since 1990. A number of state owned enterprises were privatized and most others corporatised. Systematic programmes of competitive tendering and contracting were introduced. A large part of the policy advising function, traditionally the purview of the higher Civil Service, was contracted out.

The Chief Executives of the new agencies were placed on fixed-term performance contracts with full financial and personnel authority. A senior executive service was created to facilitate the new management system with a provision to recruit outside of government. State Sector Act (1988), The Employment Contracts Act (1991), Public Finance Act (1991), and other legislation's empowered the success of reforms. The government claims that reforms are meeting most expectations. The reform literature praised the New Zealand reforms as a leading model for other nations.

The contraction of government in Australia began in 1975 but proceeded until mid 1980s. Australia relied heavily on the commercialization (contracting out) of many services. To better manage the new systems and to improve the leadership for the public service Australia established a Senior Executive Service enabling recruitment through public advertisement and competition.

Financial Reforms

Fiscal reforms agenda advocates consolidating and tightening financial discipline, reducing government budget deficit, improving tax administration, clearing government arrears, reducing subsidies through improved cost recovery and carryout funds for modest public investment and the maintenance of existing public works.

In developing countries, as in industrial countries, governments have undertaken to reduce public spending. They introduced cut backs in socio-economic programmes and resorted to improve the efficiency and effectiveness of public spending by privatizing public services or by imposing user fees. However, reduction in public spending entails political costs favouring the wealthy, at the expense of the poor and disadvantaged groups.

As a part of overall reforms different countries adopted measures of financial management: Financial Management Initiative (FMI) of the British Government under Margaret Thatcher simplified financial reporting and accounting systems. In strongly emphasized cost consciousness and clearer and stronger controls over public spending responsibility and budgets in each ministers portfolio. But its impact was stronger on the control of administrative running costs than that of programme expenditure and political considerations continued to overrule managerial rationality.

In Australia, the Financial Management Improvement Programme and Programme-Management and Budgeting emphasized the quality of service delivery as well as more simple and transparent process. There was strong emphasis on controlling the cost of government operation and eliminating the traditional bureaucratic 'inching up' of annual costs. From 1987 onwards, an efficiency dividend was exacted from departments by reducing their running cost allocation by 1.25 percent to retain much of the money saved. The departments were allowed to negotiate 'borrowings'. However, the government continues to be involved in wage setting and borrowing by public enterprises.

In New Zealand the Public Finance Act of 1989 required departments to move to a new accounting system—Which reflects the full cost of resources and enables better monitoring of efficiency.

In Norway Budget reform was implemented in 1986 and gradually extended in recent years for a more efficient governmental budget system. Budget reforms have more success in achieving greater local flexibility than in improving performance and political control.[39]

Democratization/Decentralization

Three aspects of modernity—industrialism, democracy and

nationalism have impinged on bureaucracy in the world today[40]. Bureaucracies are never democratic, instead they are administrative and hierarchic. To certain extent democratizing countries could bring them under popular control, but the modem bureaucracies have been functioning as organs of domination and exploitation. Therefore, responsible political institutions are needed that can effectively impose accountability on all the appointed officials of government. For this, it is necessary to understand how the institutions of representative governance can most effectively be organised and used to impose accountability on public bureaucracies[41].

New Public Administration movement sought to democratize bureaucracy to make it more responsive to the citizens. The fundamental problem is how to bring bureaucracy under the effective control of responsible and representative political institutions. How to transform domineering bureaucrats into responsible servants, particularly in the newly liberated countries of Asia, Africa and Latin America, Central and East European countries. The question, therefore is not how to redesign or modernize bureaucracy. Hence, the present administrative reform's main intention should be how to enhance the political control over bureaucracy by politicizing and democraticising the institutions of governance at various levels of government and state. However, the capacity of representatives and the institutions to monitor and inspire the highly professional and competent public administers is becoming increasingly problematic. Administrative reform in a way also calls for political reforms, i.e., in popular elections, political parties, elected assemblies, responsible heads of government and the rule of law[42].

Decentralization through administrative reforms reduces the distance between citizens and public administration. Decentralization effects the distribution of powers between the centre and the local authorities and effects the system of legal sources. All these issues can be resolved through reforms of decentralization if the reforms are for providing autonomy and the vision of the administration is directed towards 'customer-oriented services'. It means that there should be a shift not only from state to local authorities, but also from a bureaucratic to functional state.

The experience of last 15 years[43] shows that devolution of powers affects, political stability, public service performance, equity and macro-economic stability. However, Governments responded to demands for increased self-government by devolving power and authority to lower-tiers of government. By 1998 out of 48 largest countries 34 had held elections at both the national and local levels. Half of them not only decentralized politically but also decentralized major functional responsibilities. Due to decentralization there is substantial increases in the share of public expenditure. Now local governments account for 20 percent of government expenditure in many countries. About 95 percent of democracies have erected sub-national governments in all the countries. However, the implementation of decentralization is haphazard. Many countries gave priority to growth and administrative efficiency rather political decentralization.

One important lesson is that no strategy can stop decentralization process as the pressures to decentralize are beyond the control of governments. Everywhere, in all the continents for variety of factorsr[44]. there is insurmountable pressure for broader distribution of political power and participation in the good governance. Therefore it is wise to governments to welcome the trend and face decentralization with available past experience of different countries.

Indian Experience

While the administrative reforms were in full swing all over the world for many years, the government of India suddenly woke up and held the conference of Chief Secretaries of States on November, 20, 1996 followed by a conference of Chief Ministers in May 1997 to discuss about the crisis in Indian

Administration. It was recognised that governance has to be extended beyond traditional bureaucracies and to involve actively citizens and consumer groups to empower and inform the public and to ensure service delivery and programme execution through autonomous elected local bodies.

There was consensus for ensuring responsive, accountable, transparent, decentralised and people-friendly administration at all levels. An action plan for an Effective and Responsive Government was prepared by the Government. The Action plan consists of the following aspects:

1. Citizen's Charter and an Accountable Administration.
2. Effective and speedy public grievance redressal system.
3. Empowering elected local bodies and decentralised delivery of services.
4. Review of Laws, regulations and procedures.
5. Transparency and Right to Information.
6. Code of ethics for Public Service
7. Tackling corruption and cleansing administration.

The prime Minister of India emphasised[45] the need to make administration responsive, efficient and compassionate. He blamed largely the political class for the ills of administration. He wanted the administration to work with a sense of mission and a result-oriented approach. Along with the Prime Minister at the centres few Chief Ministers at the state level are struggling to tune the administration.

Action Plan Implementation[46]

Nothing much can be expected in such a short time of three years. However, as a part of the overall reform process it is informed that many departments have announced some sort of citizen's charters and citizen friendly initiatives. In bigger states elected local bodies have been empowered by the amendment of the Constitution. However, in many other states the power struggle is going on. It is also informed that a thorough review of the existing laws was undertaken and many laws are amended, repealed, and dropped. A number of documents are prepared along with schemes to be initiated. Some bills are pending for approval of the parliament, like Freedom of Information Bill, Bill on Electronic Data Transfer and Transaction. Finance Ministry also initiated some reforms. As a part of the Reform Agenda, the Government of India constituted a Constitutional Review Committee. Lot of debate and discussion is initiated throughout the nation particularly about the eradication of political and administrative corruption. However, there is tall talk about the reform, but the reform initiation is very little, mainly due to political instability and administrative interest.[47]

Performance Evaluation

Three general mode[48] in the light of the experience of the other countries, particularly the developing countries, the CEE and NIS are pursuing their own reforms. The evaluation of the reform performance and the implications are hereunder:

1. Reforms created new expectations for governments—achievement of expectations depended on the political commitment for change, the reform model opted, and the need and desire for reform.
2. In most cases public organizations look smaller and slimmer.
3. To a great extent the reforms restructured the public service. For example. Next Steps in UK and Senior Executive Service in Australia.
4. There is considerable improvement in the leadership of public manager/executive at different levels. NPM, HRM, invention etc. helped the process.
5. Simplification of financial management, budget coordination, increased transparency.
6. Better public management need of the reforms is

creating a new political system undesired by the reformers.

7. Will to change or design the culture (towards a new, output oriented, cost-conscious, decentralized, customer focused) of the public service is not that visible.
8. Empowerment public service users—like Citizens Charter in UK is the achievement of the reforms.
9. Business interests, the world of finance, liked the sound of government and benefited by reduction in public expenditure, deregulation and low taxation, purchase/ privatise government assets at cheaper rates, acquired government contracts to produce and deliver goods and services and expanding the volume of import and export under the liberalized
10. The public may further loose their faith in the public service if the deregulation or regulation of state bureaucracy is ineffective in containing the vested and business interests. The situation be worsened with the introduction of pro-market government bureaucracy (hiring outsiders, party advisors, former politicians and bureaucrats etc.) to carry out disinvestment programmes and make deals with private contractors (MOUs) and finalising the joint ventures. For, the mission of the newly emerging public service is not to play an active role in production, distribution, welfare and socio- economic development, but to design, facilitate regulate, monitor and evaluate the restructuring of the public sector itself. Thus, the state may weaken its legitimacy.
11. The basic norms of public service (impartiality, representativeness, equality, justice, accountability) are being replaced by commercial and market values (competitiveness, efficiency, productivity and profitability). This may lead to weaken the credibility of public interest and further challenge the legitimacy of the public service.

12. The reforms might have resulted in efficiency gains but threatened the social capital of public service and to sustain the public service as a community of trust[49], committed to pursue the public good, serving others. It raises the issues of ethics, morale, motivation, commitment, and pride of public service.
13. Downsizing, stopping recruitment, unable to attract and retain the meritorious and competent in the public service, imposing private/political consultants/advisors on the permanent policy advisors may undermine the performance of public service in meeting the emerging complex socio-economic problems.
14. It is reported that politicization of the civil service has increased in France, Australia, UK, US and other countries due to the emergence of managerialism in the public sector.
15. It is pertinent to note that the imminent changes in the administrative organization or structural adjustment programme are well publicized[50], on a global scale. The advantages and disadvantages of changes are known to the public. But, the public is divided, the administration is weakened and the political masters surrendered to the onslaught of the 'global forces" for a 'New World Order' and Global Public Administration.

    The implications of the New World Order and the emerging global public administration will likely to be more negative than positive for developing countries pushing marketization and privatization with a globally dominant public administration may develop a tendency to further empower the ruling elite[51] (the big capitalists, large land owners, big corporate powers, corrupt regimes, undemocratic and repressive forces).
16. Reforms in Australia, Britain and New Zealand gave total autonomy and responsibility to departmental heads, they moved to a system of managerial incentives based on output as a basis for performance measurement.

17. Administrative reforms, it is alleged, reduced the public accountability aspect to a technical question of designing control procedures and institutions and reforms seek change in the administrative practice without considering the accountability culture of public management[52]. Citizens Charter initiative in Britain aimed to create greater transparency in the aims, performance and delivery of government services. This is expected to strengthen local democracy by empowering people with information and increasing their interest in local affairs. The spirit of the Charter not only unites the major political parties but there are signs of an emerging consensus around the new public management.

Inspite of the political will and commitment in policy changes, legislative enactment's and executive decisions, it is still observed that the implementation of reform programmes is frequently restrained due to the absence of political consensus. In most countries a separate political group/minister at the highest level nearer to the chief executive has been entrusted with the responsibility of reform implementation[53]. However, the allocation of responsibilities between the politicians and the managers concerning reform implementation is not that clear. As such there are deficiencies in political decision-making goals of reform programmes and the management change.

It is argued that "the political leadership not only misdiagnosed the patient but also applied the wrong remedy"[54]. It requires a strong capacity to adapt and to deal with a better informed media, policy communities, interest groups and the public. Therefore, governments, it is suggested, now require a 'strong policy advisory capacity'. Political leadership ignored this aspect or even down played.

The quest for efficiency, effectiveness and economy has been the dominant impetus to administrative reforms in many countries. The reforms offered management practices and advocated smaller and less intrusive government in place of larger and more interventionist government. This quest proposed restructuring government organizations and improving efficiency by managerialist methods. The subjects of reforms are not just the institutions and procedures of civil service but also the inputs to the policy process which affect the political functions of the government. It is felt that often the need (New Zealand) or the desire (China) or need and desire (Russia) prompted to new policy directions which provided the impetus to define the functions of government and initiated to improve institutions, instruments and procedures.

Public Administration reforms in developing and transitional nations are in general directed by policy reform. The reforms are also often the result of external intervention, such as the Structural Adjustment Programme of the World Bank.

The reforms proposed to alter public administration to management, shifting the focus from inputs to outputs and outcomes. The emphasis on achieving effective outcomes induced to move towards devolution, decentralization, contracting out. The reforms intended to change the 'culture' of public administration to new public management. The NPM culture has taken root in developed countries and its wave is being spread in developing countries.

In a way the legitimacy of the public service is lessened due to cuts in size and allocations for welfare, but in another way, the legitimacy is broadened for its new orientation towards the participation of the orientation towards the participation of the customers and citizens. The reform effort of making the processes more transparent, enhanced the confidence.

International donors might have required to satisfy certain conditions through reforms but in essence the change appears to be more structural rather than functional. Therefore, there seem to be more strategies of reform than progress, particularly in developing countries.

The positive achievements of the reforms are: decentralization, downsizing, cutting red tape, HRM, more responsiveness of the higher civil service to the elected and appointed officials, merging policy and operations, changes in budgeting systems and performance measurement etc.

The strategies of the reform are not that successful in regard to: democratization, equity, empowering employees, greater autonomy, public accountability, social welfare, managing for outcomes, regulation and control.

The overall assessment of reforms is mixed. They are more incremental, not radical everywhere and less inventional, more need-based rather desired-based. The efficiency motive of the reforms should pave the way to the thinking of good governance.

REFERENCES

1. Like, Permanence, impartiality, equality, neutrality, anonymity, merit, accountability, and representativeness.
2. Like inefficiency, red-tape incompetence, unresponsiveness, tunnel vision, secrecy, isolationism, corruption etc.

3. Romzek, Barbara S. (2000), Dynamics of Public Sector Accountability in an Era of Reform, International Review of Administrative Sciences, 66:21-41.
4. Caiden, Gerald E. (1994): Administrative Reform—American Style, Public Administrative Review, 54(2): 123.
5. For details, Haque, Shamsul, M (1998) Legitimation Crisis: A Challenge for Public Service in the Next Century, International Review of Administration Sciences, 64(1): 13-26.
6. "With a certain ideological slant—very much pro-business and anti-government", *Ibid*, 124; World Bank's, World Development Report, 1996, Toward Better and Slimmer Government.
7. Caiden, Gerald E.: Administrative Reform Comes of Age, 1991, Walter de Gruyter, Berlin.
8. Ingraham, Patricia, W. (1997): Play it Again, Sam; It is Still not Right; Searching for the Right Notes in Administrative Reform, Public Administration Review, 57(4): 325-331.
9. Wilenski, Peter, (1986): Administrative Reform—General Principal and the Australian Experience, Public Administration, 64, Autumn: 257.
10. Politt, Christopher (1996): Antistatist Administrative Reforms

and New Administrative Directions: Public Administration in the United Kingdom. Public Administration Review, 56 (I): 82-84.
11. *Ibid.*
12. The Main Theoretical Sources were Monetarism, Austrian School of Economics, Public Choice Theory and Libertarian Philosophy.
13. Bill Clinton and Al Gore in USA, (1992), The Labour Party in Australia, 1983 contested elections promising administrative reforms.
14. Haque, Shamul, M. (1998): Legitimation Crisis: A Challenge for Public Service in the Next Century, International Review of Administrative Sciences, 64, (I): 15.
15. Margaret Thatcher, Ronald Reagon, Jim Carter, Brian Mulroney and others in UK, USA and Canada.
16. Renu Khotor, Managing the Environment in An Interdependent World, in Jean-Calude Garcia-Zamor & Renu Khotor (Eds.) (1995), Public Administration in the Global Village. Praeger, West Port: 83-98.
17. Osborne David and Gaebler Ted (1992): Reinventing Government: How the Entrepreneurial Spirit is Transforming the Public Sector, Addison-Welsey.
18. For details, Brudney, Jeffrey L., Hebert F. Ted and Wright Deil S. (1999): Reinventing Government in the American States: Measuring and Explaining Administrative Reform, Public Administration Review, 99 (1): 19-30.
19. *Ibid.*, 28-29.
20. Ingraham, Patricia (1997): Play it Again, Sam; It is still not right: Searching for the right notes in Administrative Reform, Public Administration Review, 57,(4): 325-331. 'Managerialist' administrative reforms in the UK, Australia, New Zealand and USA are evaluated in this article.
21. Davies, Morton (1998): Civil Servants, Managerialism and Democracy, International Review of Administrative Sciences, 64; 129.
22. Hood, C.C.: A Public Management for all Seasons, Public Administration, 69, (Spring):3-17.
23. Masser, Kai: Public Sector Administrative Reforms. The International Encyclopaedia of Public Policy and Administration: 1851-52.
24. Aucin, P. (1990): Administrative Reforms in Public Management:

Paradigms, Principles. Paradoxes and Pendulums, Governance, 3: 115-137.

25. Australian Management Advisory Board (1993), an oversight group was created for public service reform.
26. The energy and commitment of public managers needs to be more powerfully mobilized. See for details, Ian Marsh, Programme Strategy and Coalition Building as Facets of New Public Management, Australian Journal of Public Administration, 58 (4): 54-67.
27. Klages, Helmut and Loffler, Elke (1998): New Public Management in Germany: The Implementation process of the New Steering Model, International Review of Administrative Sciences, 64:41-54 and Ridley F.F. (1996): The New Public Management in Europe: Comparative perspectives, public policy and administration, 11, (1): 16-29.
28. Ewan Ferile, Andrew Pettigrew, Lynn Ashburner, Louise Fitzerald, (1996): The New Public Management in Action, OUP.
29. For the classification of the role of the state, see, Masser Kai, *op. cit.*: 1855-1857.
30. Bennett Sara and Muralidharan V.R., (January 8, 2000), "New Public Management and Health Care in Third World", Economic and Political Weekly: 59-68.
31. Kaul, M. (1997): "The New Public Administration: Management Innovations in Government, Public Administration and Development, 17: 13-26.
32. Barbara Wake Caroll and David E. Garkut, Is there empirical evidence of a trend towards 'managerialism'? A longitudinal study of six countries, Canadian Public Administration, 39(4): 535-533.
33. Aucin, Peter, The New Public Management: Canada in Comparative Perspective, 1995, Montreal, Institute for Research on Public Policy, 246-56.
34. For details, Quiggin, John (1999): The Future of Government: Mixed Economy or Minimal State?, Australian Journal of Public Administration, 58(4): 39-53.
35. *Ibid*, p-41.
36. The motives and consequences of privatization are well explained by Farazmand, Ali, (1999): Privatization or reform? Public Enterprise management in transition. International Review of Administrative Services, 65: 551-567.
37. For details, O'Toole, Barry J. and Jordan Grant (Eds.), (1995):

Next Steps: Improving Management in Government? Dartmouth, Aldershot.

38. For details, Boston, Jonathan, Lessons from the Antipodes, in O'Toole, J. Barry and Jordan Grant (Eds.) (1995), *op. cit.*, 161-177.
39. Tomm Christensen and Per Loegried (1998): Administrative Reform Policy: The Case of Norway, International Review of Administrative Sciences, 64: 457-475.
40. Riggs, Fred. W., Modernity and Bureaucracy, (1997): Public Administration Review, 57(4): 347-353.
41. *Ibid.*, 349.
42. Stowe, Kenneth (1992): Good Piano Won't Play Bad Music: Administrative Reform and Good Governance, Public Administration 70 (Autumn): 387-394.
43. The existing situation around the World is analyzed at length by World Development Report, 1999/2000, Entering the 21st Century, Oxford University Press, New York, 2000: 45-50 and 107-124.
44. The Emergence Modern Economics, the Rise of the urban, literate middle class, decline military threats etc. World Development Report, 1999-2000: 124.
45. Vajpayee, Atal Bihari (1999): Indian Administration Today, Remedying its Weaknesses, Indian Journal of Public Administration. XLV (I): 1-4.
46. Jha Nikhilesh, (1999): Effective and Responsive Government Regulatory Reform Initiatives of Union Government, Indian Journal of Public Administration. XLV, (2): 240-249.
47. For more details. Action Plan for an Effective and Responsive Government, Department of Administrative Reforms and Public Grievances, Government of India, 1998, Indian Journal of Public Administration, July-Sept. 1998: 626-660.
48. Incremental model of US, Staged model in Australia and UK, Fresh Start model of New Zealand, the later addressed the more fundamental political and administrative issues and have shown that political leadership is important, not political rhetoric to build a new government.
49. For details see, Gregory, Robert J. (1999): Social Capital Theory and Administrative Reform, Maintaining Ethical Probity in Public Service, Public Administration Review, 59(1): 63-71.
50. But also the reformers determined to push the changes through; therefore, to reduce the resistance, the reformers, held series of

negotiations with their potential opponents and managed them. This is the fundamental lesson of the new reforms, Polidano Charles, *op. cit.*, 468.

51. Farazmand Ali, *op. cit.*, 81.
52. Ramzek, Barbaro, *op. cit.*, 37-40.
53. All reform programmes of Margaret Thatcher and John Major in UK were supervised from the Prime Minister's office and a separate department in the Ministry of Finance was responsible for the reforms.
54. Peters B. Guy and Donald J. Saroie (1994): Civil Service Reform, Misdiagnosing the Patient, Public Administration Review, 54 (5): 418-425.

12

The Trauma of Contemporary Public Administration

MOHIT BHATTACHARYA

The field of Public Administration has been very active in recent times, and with changes in the role of Government globally, Public Administration is currently engaged in some sort of soul-searching. Today, some of the major theoretical concerns, apparently contradictory are:

(a) Application of Public choice theory to Public Administration, posing market Vs. State debate as contending providers of public good.
(b) Decentralisation and democracy-enhancing institutional measures at the work place and gross-root level empowerment of the people.
(c) Thorough scrutiny of the Weberian theory of bureaucracy; 'rational bureaucracy' being assailed as self-aggrandizing, priority-distorting and budget maximizing.
(d) Organizational pluralism, suggesting that let the consumers 'choose' and no more of 'imposed' organisations. As a consequence, suggestions are being offered for load-shedding of Government, privatization, decentralization and people empowerment, encourage-

ment of NGOs in the voluntary sector. Organization pluralism is manifesting itself in the advocacy of social capacity as against Governmental capability.

Government through the Agency of the Public Administration is being treated as just one form of Governance. The concept of 'governance' opens up possibilities of Government through non-bureaucratic agencies (other than pure Government).

(e) 'Performance Partnership' in the form of different levels coming together like Public-Private Joint effort. And networking of Government, NGO, Private Agencies is being pursued and suggested.

(f) Small Government in terms of down-sizing and grass-roots people's efforts is yet another idea being broached now. In this context, decentralization of Government and people's own efforts are being more and more advocated. Another kindred suggestion is the re-conceptualization of Government's role: steering, policy-orientation, "enabling rather than doing". Also, re-examination and assertion of 'Public Interest' has led to a revival of interest in this core concept. Neo-institutionalism in the form of institutional capacity-binding is being advocated, and institutional studies are having field day.

Current Scenario

Public Administration today is reflecting in large part the changing nature of practice of Governments especially in the developed world. The practices of traditional Public Administration have come under increasing attack form neo-liberal economists, interest group theorists and rational choice scholars who have provided the intellectual ammunition for respective politicians determined to reduce the size and scope of the public sector. This is scarcely surprising since the theoretical change have tended to emphasise the significant extent to which Public Administration is political and is part of the overall process of determining 'who gets what'. Approaches to Public Administration are also embedded in wider conceptions of the State, the relationship between State and market and of citizenship. Changes in the ideological climate are, therefore, likely to impact upon Public Administration.

Multiple Models of Governance

Public Administration has from its inception, witnessed periodic changes in dominant conceptionalizations about what Government does. Waves of reforms have swept through the public sector over the past several decades under societal pressures and demands—both national and international. These changes have been piecemeal and fragmented without being integrated into clear 'visions' regarding planned change in Government. The *market model* of Governance has been holding centre-state since the eighties; but there have been other models alongside it which have been equally powerful and deserve careful consideration (B. Guy Peters, "Models of Governance for the 1990s", in Donald F. Kettl and H. Brinton Milward (eds.), The State of Public Management, The Johns Hopking University Press, Baltimore and London, 1996). For instance, the *'participatory model'* that concentrates on the participation of lower echelons of workers and even the clients and the citizenry has been a direct rebuttal of the traditional hierarchic, bureaucratic model in Public Administration. There has been the other type of *'flexible Government'* idea that goes against the conventional model of permanent employment. Public organisations with much less full-time permanent employees, and increasing level of part-time and temporary workers has steadily come into existence at many places depending on the nature of the labour market. Still another model has been the *'deregulating Government'* idea which one can immediately trace to 'reinventing Government' idea which one can immediately trace to 'reinventing Government' (a la Osborne and Gaebler). As it has been put:

"The politicians of the 1980s appeared to have a special dislike and destruct of the public bureaucracy and they sought to curtail its power over policy. The assumption of deregulating Government is that if some of the constraints on action were eliminated, Government could perform its current functions more efficiently and it might be able to undertake new and creative activities to improve the collective welfare of the society". The deregulating model rests on the belief that public interest would be better served by a more active and interventionist public sector, and in this perspective, collective action is part of the solution and not part of the problem for contemporary societies (as was being alleged by public choice theorists).

What emerges at the end of the debate is a more flexible and open-ended vision of Governance. "As long as democracy is valued", as it has been so ably put, "the big questions of Public Administration must go beyond the big questions of Public Management" (John, J. Kirlin, "The Big Question in a Democracy", Public Administration Review, September, October, 1996). Public Administration cripples its role in society if understood primarily in terms of managing public agencies. Minnowbrook-I and Blacksburg Manifesto have both raised this issue of democratic Governance in public interest. What is relevant in the context of the Third World is that Public Administration is being crippled in the name of 'structural adjustment', invoking more and more the 'market model' of Governance. The 'interests' of Public Administration are no longer people-related; these are instead capital-related. And here lies the perils of externally induced administrative 'reform' through which most third world countries are passing today.

In terms of administrative theory-building, the current emphasis on 'public management' *via* the market model of Governance needs to be viewed in proper historical perspective. Historically, two contrasting visions have guided the pursuit of administration analysis: *the managerial vision* and *the democratic vision*. Both public bureaucracy (and managerialism) and democratic polity are needed in a liberal-democratic society. But, administration analysts since the days of Wilson and the authors of POSDCORB have often been tempted to over-emphasise 'managerialism' with its prediction for efficiency, economy and effectiveness. The other more central pursuits of Public Administration like achieving a democratic polity, improving the instruments of collective action and creating condition for good citizenship and increasing societal learning are of no concern for the 'public management' advocates. A major flaw in the managerial perspective is its inordinate interest in organizational concerns and measures of organiza-tional performance. The interests of a democratic polity and maintenance of a legal order are substituted by the concern for organizational survival. There is in this move a misplaced emphasis on 'instrument' at the cost of 'purpose'. Public Administration as 'management' misses altogether the overarching perspective of a democratic polity. Sustained capacity of the political system for collective action, effective citizenship and developing and nurturing the civic infrastructure for protecting citizens' rights and promoting collective life are of vital significance for any public administrative system in a democracy. The new 'management' cult is particularly ominous for the Third World Public Administration, as it tends to strengthen 'bureaucracy' further, impeding the development of alternative people's institution so necessary for both generating social capacity to govern and creating more democratic spaces outside of central bureaucratic administration.

13

Role of Government in Changing Economic Scenario in India: New Public Management Approach

NEELIMA DESHMUKH

The whole world has entered into 21st Century in unsettled and complex environment, posing challenges well as opportunities for us. We are facing new and serious challenges from the forces of nationalism, fundamentalism, intolerance, separatism and economic and political upheavals especially in the third world countries, which are already burdened, with problems of development as a crucial issue. Most of them are struggling with removal of poverty, illiteracy and combating with ever swelling population. "The challenge of the development in the broadest sense is to improve the quality of life. Especially in world's poor Countries. better quality of life generally calls for higher income that involves much more. It encompasses as ends in themselves better education, high standards of health & nutrition, less poverty, cleaner environment, more equality of opportunity, greater individual freedom and rich cultural life."[1]

In brief the development could be defined as a process aimed at improving well being of people, raising their standard of living improving their education, health and also opening out new opportunities for richer and more varied life. Better health with longer life and less sickness is crucial to better standard of living.

The 21st Century on one hand brought many revolutionary technological developments in wide range of areas have radically changed the production of goods and services. Programmes in the fields of information and technology, telecommunications, electronics, biotechnology. chemistry, medicine have opened unparallel opportunities for the humanity. On the other hand too many people remain excluded from these development leaving under very difficult conditions. Fruits are developments are reaped by the upper crust of few. whole heaps of people are deprived of basic facilities even. In short trickle down approach has not attained mentionable desired results.

India is emerging fast as a super nation. We have nuclear weapons to create pressure on international community but still many of us do not have access to clean drinking water and sanitation are the basic needs of life. "Around half of world's population is living below poverty line. Two billion people lack access to clear drinking water, 800 million people suffer from hunger, 500,000 mothers die every year while giving birth to babies, 30,000 children per day die of malnutrition, and other preventable causes."[2]

Most of these problems could have otherwise been tackled, but poor remains excluded from the fruits of development. With this background of paradoxes, the government needs to address major problems, and analyse the situation in changing economic scenario in the perspectives of,

- How to build institutional frame-work of economics and social policies, conducive to stand and effective social development.
- Role of Public Administration vis-à-vis State in ensuring universal nutrition, access to health, service and education.

- Public policy to meet immense challenges concerning inequity and to provide opportunities for socially excluded.
- Role of school of Public Administration in fighting the agencies of poverty and social exclusion.

"Third of people are below poverty line which means their daily income is less than a dollar. Minimum earning required as per World Bank criteria to live above poverty, i.e., 30 US dollar per month. Average earning of an Indian is 440 US dollar per year amounting to Rs. 1727 in Indian currency. Number of people living below poverty line is 300 million (30 crores) with almost same number of unemployed persons. 27 million people are working in organized sector, 40 millions registered as unemployed. Those working in organized public sector as State or Center are about 19 million (1.9 crores) 8 millions (0.8 crores) in organized private sector and 320 millions (32 crores) in unorganized sector"[3] The nation needs to create at least 10 million (1 crore) jobs every year to fulfil aspirations of Indian citizens.

With the LPG, the economic scenario in the Indian context is discouraging. The industries are facing grave recession, and failures, most of the units are sick, farmers are committing suicide, because of their failures to compete at international level. It is in this background the government needs revise its role, restructure the processes, behaviour and approach in response to changing scenario. On the other hand the governments institutions, the wings of the carrier of development to the grass root level should adopt the appropriate model and shift its paradigm towards New Public Management, (NPM).

Presently almost 76 per cent of budgetary allocations are spent on salary and establishment, leaving no money for development activities. Though our country has improved its rank from 127 in terms of human development index in 2000 to 103 in 2004 calls our attention to various administrative reforms in particular aimed at its all round development which is an open society with closed mindset in contrast voraciously developing China closed society with open mind. Governance has collapsed and many unfinished tasks are left over, growth and development have been disproportionate, e.g., Keral a state with more human development whereas in it is more growth but less human development.

"It is a Country with 17 per cent of World's Human resource. 0.6 per cent of the World's trade and only 1.3 per cent of World's GDP. We need to become resource base for world market, since 98.7 per cent of the World's buying powers i.e., 99.4 per cent World's trade lies not with India,"[4] GDP needs to be raised from present status of 6.5 to 8 but the various constraints as:

- Unsuitable export, import policies.
- Labour Problems.
- Slow down/Stoppage of Industries.
- Neglected rural industrial development.
- Disheartening Banking Scenario.
- Too many procedural formalities, leading to red tapism, now reduced from 97 to 43.
- Blockades at the level of official and non officials relations.
- Politics as a game of manipulation for vested interests.
- Large size Government structure, which needs to be downsized.
- Right work attitude/work culture.
- Time killing Committee system.
- No innovations from 1996.
- Representative/participatory democracy.
- 30 per cent—Low voter turn out 222.
- Lack of massive Political Administrative, Educational Reforms.
- Corruption and political instability.
- No provision for infrastructure in budget.

- Create more and more hindrances in the passage of development.

These present challenges make the NPM application inevitable to situation In the era of LPG, particularly the Indian Government is expected to play the role of Cybernetic state meaning which:

- Government as facilitator.
- Goal oriented.
- Efficiency as the guiding force.
- Decentralized decision-making.
- Accuracy.
- Greater technological skills.
- De bureaucratization.
- Accessibility of information.
- Broaden effective participation.
- Better communication.
- Transparency.
- Enlargement of people's choice.
- Paperless Administration.

The focus of the 21st century is going to on numerous developments. Therefore the government is expected to be cybernetic state where in it functions as servo mechanics conjoining the polity and economy to achieve public objective. Public policies should be designed in such a way as to meet the immense challenges concerning in equality and to provide for the opportunities to socially excluded. The government should be reinvented, in the Indian context, as per David Osborne and Ted Gaebler's 10 principles listed as follows:

- Catalytic Government.
- Community oriented.
- Competitive Government.
- Mission driven.

- Result oriented.
- Customer driven.
- Enterprising.
- Anticipatory Government.
- Decentralized and market oriented.

Governance revolves around finance structures hence the fiscal deposits are to be managed and improved by making effective tax collection making it more sustainable. We need to make:

- Quantum change in the level of development.
- Change in mindset.
- Red tapism should go.
- Electoral reforms, better increases participation of public, strengthening democracy.
- New leadership with vision and planning.
- Spreading technology to rural masses and last man down to the earth.
- Policy designs to be altered.
- Abandonment of committee system.
- Government downsizing.
- Changes in the economic policies of many parts of the world, including India calls for the changes in politics and political culture.
- Management of resources should be skillful and first concern.
- More concentration in human resources.
- Professionalism.
- Cross cultural values.
- International finances be approved.
- Guarantee of social security problem.

High incomes and efficient organizations do not automatically translate into better human lives. Therefore the institutions, basically local self-government needs to be restructured with tailor made redesigned policies, ensuring its effective implementation on to cope up with administrative failures, such as:

- Diseconomy: Results are achieved at unnecessary high cost.
- Counter productive: Results are contrary to those desired.
- Ineffectiveness: Responses evoked are mere rearrangement of inputs and outputs achieving little or nothing.
- Tail Chasing: The larger the quantum, higher the demand.

New Public Management Approach Application to Local Governments: An Essential Factor

Considering the shift of the government's role from police to welfare to develop the states, more and more attempts have been made to revitalize and institutionalize the local government in systematic way through various reforms and constitutional amendments with democratic decentralization as its sole in true spirits so as to ensure the contribution to the process of the nation building. During this face lifting exercise of developing societies, the oppressed class of the society, the women backward people from SC/ST categories could no longer be neglected and become the focus of envisaging potentials, while empowering people and assuring increased public participation in democratic way. Owing to the noble intentions of implementing community development programme

1. Suitable administrative decentralization
2. Placement of decentralized administrative system under the effective control of elected representatives became the under current shaping Indian polity. By way of 73rd and 74th constitutional amendments 1993,

relating to urban bodies respectively has gained greater impor-tance, particularly the Panchayati Raj institutions because the large strata of Indian populace resides in rural area, calling for better attention at the grass root level, which is a three-tier structure and real scenario of Indian rural governance, catering to the development needs as a administrative wing of administration.

The root cause of every developmental problem hinges around continuous financial paucity, which becomes a main constant if these PRIs. The sources of income of these local bodies are very meagre, most of the times the tax collection through various sources are extremely low and ultimately these bodies become slowly solely dependent on grants-in-aid. Since the financial strings are controlled by central government, the center-state relations play very important role in accessing required proportion of finances for the development work and infrastructural Setup.

Identifying this factor 73rd-74th amendments provided for independent finance commission at center and state level which are mainly responsible for

1. Distribution of development funds to rural and urban bodies from the net proceeds of the tax duties, tolls and fees leviable by the state which may be divided between them end the allocation between Panchayats at all levels of their respective shares of such proceeds.
2. Determination of taxes, tolls, duties and fees, which may be, assign to or appropriated by Panchayats and grant-in-aid from the consolidated funds of India in proportion to their populations and backlog. Furthermore the population as per 1991 census, the world banks development parameters 1991 has been adopted when the bill of 73rd and 74th amendment act was passed in the same year.

All activities revolve around finances, which are controlled by these finance commissions. Different parameters are needed to allocate the share amongst the rural and urban local bodies, in addition to the availability and data collection at the local level. On the basis of which sharing could be made. SFC's should integrate both plan and non-plan expenditure in the process of resources transference to local bodies strengthening its role. This further implies that the proper methods logical framework is needed for making transference process simple and transparent. The present situation of local resource mobilization is very disheartening. Typically local bodies are lacking in sufficient self-mobilized sources. The dependency on the grants is very high. Under the circumstances local bodies can hardly perform the assigned task in more effective way. So not only large amount of grant-in-aid to be allocated progressively but also resource mobilization at local levels has to be put on the topmost priority in the agenda of state finance commission. Therefore NPM philosophy should be immediately applied to these state finance commission, strengthening them further

- Provide more authority to local institutions.
- Change in the pattern revenue distribution criteria.
- PRIs, dependency syndrome (on government grant in aid).
- Functions and power of PRIs are mismatched.
- Criteria for resource distribution between Center and State also to be redesigned.
- Tardy growth of SFCs and their working pattern calls for a change; only 16 SFCs are functioning all over 22 States ill developed specially in north side in state like Bihar SFCs are not formed at all.
- Grants should be predictable, in amount and timing of transfer.
- Simplicity in formula for transferring intergovernmental resources, ensuring transparency.

- Autonomy for fiscal discipline and own resource mobilization.
- Efficiency: the transfer mechanism should not only become gap-filling approach.
- Promotion of incentives: There should be adequate built in arrangements for encouraging resources mobilization and penalizing for wastage and uneconomic parties.

Conclusion

Globalization is a buzzword. It is not a new concept but as age-old like Christianity. In fact the interweaving factor of production and consumption and life style cutting across territorial boundaries. In fact Liberalisation, Privatisation and Globalisation (LPG) era is same old wine in new bottle in the form of hegemonic power which leads to sharping inequalities and regional disparities. Only well placed ones can take the advantage of structural Adjustment Programme (SAP) but the poor are deprived. At present society is at unrest, surrounded by the mystery of inefficiency, rampant corruption and apathy of the government institutions to deliver the goods and services to public. All said and done, restructuring and empowering these government institutions are absolutely essential to face the changing economic scenario.

Performance in terms of output criteria must relate to formulation and implementation of public policies, the authority and effectiveness of public institutions and their accountability for results. Huntington is very right when in the very opening sentence of his book he says: "The most important political distinction among countries concern not their form government, but their degree of government."[8]. The degree of government must be interpreted to mean both the effectiveness and the scope of public authority and extensive political responsibility for public matter.

A conspicuous example of failure in civic co-operation is provided by the local bodies in general and the Panchayati institutions in particular. Panchayats have virtually become the despair of all those who set value on democratic development. The Panchayat institutions have failed both as institutions of self-government and local development.

Suggestions

In order to overcome the problems and intricacies faced by the Finance Commission it is suggested that it should adopt the following criteria for recommending the transfer of resources.

(1) *Ensure the Autonomy*: Presently not only the PRIs but also other urban local bodies are known for their dependency syndrome. As the essence of the decentralization is self-rule and autonomy the fiscal discipline and own resource mobilization should be encouraged as a key to autonomy.

(2) *Equity*: The well known dictum of equity, i.e., "from each according to one's own ability and to each according to one's needs" is relevant in considering resource mobilization arc intergovernmental resource transfers as well. It should be noted that Panchayats at all levels are very unequal in size, resources, and development attainments. Given the extreme disparities, decentralization in such conditions can produce completely different results.

(3) *Predictability*: The PRIs should know the amount and the timings of the transfer of the funds to make provision for planning, budgeting and the implementation of their activities. Irregular payments are not conducive to efficiency. Many a times the allocations may not even be paid resulting in overdues which may be a permanent loss to them.

(4) *Efficiency*: The resource transfer should be so designed as to facilitate efficient management and discourage inefficient and un-economic practices. The transfer mechanism should not turn out to be a gap filling mechanism.

(5) *Absorptive Capacity*: The resource transfer should be in tune with the utilization capacity, including availability of personnel of the receiving Panchayats.

(6) *Simplicity and Transparency*: The formula for transferring the intergovernmental resources should be simple and transparent.

Santhanam Committee (1963) has underscored the need for financial and administrative autonomy and integrated approach, the report stated thus "it is essential for stability and growth of these institutions that they should have substantial and growing resources which ore entirely with in their power to exploit and develop".

The 73rd Constitutional Amendment has not only given a constitutional status to PRIs but also defined them as a Institutions of Self-Government (Article 243) since the taxation powers of central *a*nd state government are listed as LIST I & II respectively. There is no mention of the local list for the local bodies they can have only those powers which the state govt. devolves upon them from their own taxation powers listed in item 45 to 66 of the State List which refers to empowerment of Panchayats by the state to levy taxes, duties, toll, etc. is the only enabling provision. The actual devolution rest upon the State government having no independent power of taxation. The only consolations being the constitution of State Finance Commission every 5 years. But again the role of SFC is limited as it can not create resources but can only make the recommendations regarding the sharing of resources between various levels. Implementation of these recommendation is again left to the state government which may or may not accept the same. Hence it is suggested that in order to strengthen PRIs further amendment should be made in the clause of Finance commission which is the dire need of the hour.

The democratic governance of India implies as under:

1. Periodic elections of the majority by the majority but not for majority.
2. Structure of citizens rights irrespective of caste, creed, religion.

3. Democratic structure is getting increasingly less liberalised. Economic liberalisation is coming fast in deliberalised society.
4. New opportunities are floating around.
5. Restructuring of the present democratic structure aimed at good governance.
6. Necessary elections through set of inviolable rights/ disjunction of seat/votes inadequate. Keeping in mind these consequences the political institutions should adopt themselves to Paradigms of New Public Management with human relations approach. In the changing scenario, it is inferred that the society is at unrest. surrounded by the mysteries of rampant corruption, inefficiency and apathy of the political institutions to deliver the goods and services to public, they feel suffocated with their survival at stake therefore with the changing scenario, the role of political institutions is also changed, and for meeting the changed role, effectively, these institutions and their representative should inculcate positive administrative and political culture, with value based attitude. Changes for the better are desired in the pattern of governance,

    1. Schedule XI of 73rd amendment act is not fully effective in real sense because of the decentralization has been handed, devolution has not taken place, in practice. Transparency, efficiency, are yet strange factors being dominated by corruption.
    2. Empowerment of local government.
    3. Effective tackling of gender issues.
    4. Poverty situation.
    5. Skill, technology, market level.
    6. Shrinking role of government and large role to non-government sector.
    7. Downsizing the government PSUs and giving lot of work to non-government Sector.

8. Government machinery not fully tuned up to live up to current reality.
9. During the negotiations in 1994 WTO created various agreements, which are not implemented, included large number of subject enforcement body, if country feels it can approach them for arbitration in case of non-feasibilities.
10. 56 per cent of population depends on agriculture sector contributing 25 per cent, one of the fallout

Contributors

1. S.P. Verma (Retd.) Professor of Public Administration, 54, Sahyog Apptts. Mayur Vihar, Phase-1, New Delhi-110091.
2. Noorjahan Bava (Retd.), Professor of Political Science, 140 PKT, B-SFs, DDA Flats, Sukhdev Vihar, New Delhi-110025.
3. V. Bhaskara Rao (Retd.) Professor of Public Administratrion, H.No. 1-7-454, Revenue Colony, Hanamakoda, Warangal-506001 (AP).
4. Ramesh K. Arora (Retd.) Professor of Public Administration presently visiting Professor, H.C.M. Rajasthan State Institute of Public Administration, Jawaharlal Nehru Marg, Jaipur.
5. Ashok Sharma, Professor of Public Administration, Deptt. of Public Administration, University of Rajasthan, Jaipur.
6. Neelima Deshmukh, Reader, Deptt. of Public Administration, Nagpur University, Nagpur.
7. Srinibas Pathi, Reader, Deptt. of Public Administration, Mizoram University, Aizawl.
8. R.K. Sapru (Retd.) Professor of Public Administration, University of Pubjab, Chandigarh.
9. P.M. Bora (Retd.) Professor of Public Administration, Samayak, 24, Builders Society, Nandan Colony, Aurangabad.

10. Inderajeet Singh Sodhi, Lecturer, Deptt. of Public Administration and Political Sceince, St. Wilfred College, Jaipur-20.

11. Arvind K. Sharma, Former Vice Chancellor, Mizoram University, B-948, Palam Vihar, New Gurgaon.

12. R.N. Prasad, Ex Professor and Head, Department of Public Administration and Dean, School of Social Sciences, Mizoram University, Aizawl, presently, B-183, Sainik Nagar (Uttam Nagar), New Delhi-110059.

13. Mohit Bhattacharya, Ex Vice-Chancellor University of Burdwan, Burdwan (W.B.). presently, Purvanchal, Cluster-VIII, Block K-6, Saltlake, Calcutta-700091.

Index